William Collins · The Poems

Anglistica & Americana

A Series of Reprints Selected by
Bernhard Fabian, Edgar Mertner,
Karl Schneider and Marvin Spevack

137

1973

GEORG OLMS VERLAG
HILDESHEIM · NEW YORK

WILLIAM COLLINS

THE POEMS

Edited by Walter C. Bronson
(1898)

1973

GEORG OLMS VERLAG
HILDESHEIM · NEW YORK

Note
The present facsimile is reproduced from a copy in the
possession of the Library of the University of Heidelberg.
Shelfmark: G 8262 1.

M. S.

Nachdruck der Ausgabe Boston, Mass. 1898
Printed in Germany
Herstellung: fotokop wilhelm weihert kg, Darmstadt
ISBN 3 487 04665 2

THE ATHENÆUM PRESS SERIES

G. L. KITTREDGE AND C. T. WINCHESTER

GENERAL EDITORS

The

Athenæum Press Series.

This series is intended to furnish a library of the best English literature from Chaucer to the present time in a form adapted to the needs of both the student and the general reader. The works selected are carefully edited, with biographical and critical introductions, full explanatory notes, and other necessary apparatus.

FLAXMAN'S BAS-RELIEF OF COLLINS.

From a photograph of the original in Chichester Cathedral. The poet is represented
as reading the New Testament (see pp. xxiv, xxvi), while his ode
on the Passions lies neglected on the floor.

Athenæum Press Series

THE

POEMS OF WILLIAM COLLINS

EDITED WITH INTRODUCTION AND NOTES

BY

WALTER C. BRONSON, A.M.

PROFESSOR OF ENGLISH LITERATURE IN BROWN UNIVERSITY

BOSTON, U.S.A.

GINN & COMPANY, PUBLISHERS

The Athenæum Press

1898

TO MY MOTHER

PREFACE.

———o·o:o:o·o———

THE need for a new edition of Collins is obvious. Dyce's
edition, in many ways so admirable, has long been out of
print. The Aldine *Collins*, with many merits, yet leaves
much to be desired. Of the other current editions even
the best lay no claim to originality or comprehensiveness,
while the worst are almost incredibly careless reprints of
careless predecessors. The present edition is at least of
broader scope than any which has hitherto appeared. It
contains (1) a critical text carefully transcribed from the
original editions; (2) variant readings, with their sources
and comparative value set forth; (3) numerous notes,
including a good deal of new illustrative material; (4) a
biographical sketch based so far as possible upon original
records (newly verified) and the statements of the poet's
contemporaries, the sources and their relative trustworthiness being indicated ; (5) a comprehensive and systematic
study of the poetry of Collins.

In poems which exist in more than one form, the text that
seems to represent the poet's last revision has been adopted,
other readings being given a place at the foot of the page.
The capitalization of the original editions, in which nearly
every noun begins with a capital, has been abandoned for
modern usage. Punctuation has been changed as little as
possible, but when the sense required I have not hesitated to
repoint freely; in the few instances where the meaning may
fairly be considered doubtful, either the original punctuation
has been retained or the change has been recorded in the

notes. Breathings and accents have been affixed to quotations in Greek. In some of the odes, divisional headings have been supplied where they were omitted in the original edition or were indicated by figures only. Foot-notes signed " C." are by Collins.

It is a pleasant duty to acknowledge my obligations to the friends and strangers who have aided me in this work. To the authorities of the Harvard University Library, of the British Museum, and of the South Kensington Museum I am indebted for access to original editions and collateral material; to the curates of St. Peter's the Great and the Church of St. Andrew, Chichester, for opportunity to examine the parish records of Collins's baptism and burial; to the Warden of Winchester College, for transcripts of the records of Collins's admission and superannuation at that school, with other particulars; to the Vice-Chancellor, the President of Magdalen College, the Keeper of the Archives, and Professor A. S. Napier,—all of Oxford University,—for transcripts of the university records regarding Collins and for other courtesies; to Professor Frank M. Bronson, of the Academy of Chicago University, for the translations (not otherwise accredited) from the Greek and Latin, and for most of the accompanying notes; to Professors John M. Manly, Francis G. Allinson, and Joseph N. Ashton, and Mr. R. E. Neil Dodge, now or formerly my colleagues in Brown University, and to Professor Francis B. Gummere, of Haverford College, for assistance upon sundry points; and to Dr. Daniel H. Fuller, formerly First Assistant Physician in the McLean Hospital for the Insane, for an opinion on the causes and nature of Collins's insanity. To Professor George L. Kittredge, who has read the whole book in manuscript and in proof, I wish to express my special thanks for many valuable criticisms and suggestions.

W. C. B.

PROVIDENCE, R. I., Sept. 30, 1898.

CONTENTS.

————o·o¦o·o——

CONTENTS.

INTRODUCTION.

———o○°⊙°○o———

I. THE LIFE OF COLLINS.[1]

WILLIAM COLLINS was born at Chichester, in the south of England, in the year 1721. He was baptized on Jan. 1, 1722,[2] and the tradition is that his birth occurred on the preceding Christmas. The Collins family were established in Chichester as tradesmen of the higher class in the sixteenth century. It is said that Thomas Collins, mayor of the city in 1619, was a direct ancestor of the poet.[3] The poet's

[1] The quotations from Johnson are taken from his life of Collins in the *Lives of the Poets*. The quotations from Ragsdale, T. Warton, and White are taken from letters by them. White's letter, dated Jan. 20, 1781, appeared first in *The Gentleman's Magazine* for January, 1781; it was there anonymous, but in the Aldine *Collins* it is reprinted from the original and ascribed to White on evidence in the manuscript. The letters of Ragsdale and Warton were written to William Hymers, of Oxford, who was collecting material for a new edition of Collins; they were first printed, after Hymers's death, in *The Reaper*, which was originally published (says Dyce) in *The York Chronicle* from January, 1796, to June, 1797, and was reprinted in book form, though never published, in 1798. The letters were reprinted (that by Ragsdale shamefully mutilated) in *The Gleaner*, edited by Nathan Drake (London, 1811, vol. IV, pp. 475–484) ; Ragsdale's letter was correctly reprinted in *The Monthly Magazine* for July, 1806. Ragsdale's letter is dated July, 1783. Warton's letter must have been written about the same time.

[2] " William ye. Son of William Collins then Mayor of this City & Elizabeth his wife was baptiz'd : 1 Jany." — Parish Register of the Subdeanery Church, otherwise St. Peter's the Great. The year is 1721 Old Style, *i.e.*, 1722 New Style, as the entries after March 24 show.

[3] *A History of the Western Division of the County of Sussex*, by James

father, William Collins, a hatter, filled the office of mayor in 1714 and 1721.[1] He seems to have been a man of some property; his house in East Street, which is still standing, is a large and substantial structure of brick and stone. Collins's parents had reached middle age at the time of his birth, his mother being about forty years old and his father forty-seven. Two daughters, Elizabeth and Anne, some sixteen and fifteen years older than the poet, were, so far as is known, the only other children.

It is probable that in his boyhood Collins attended the prebendal school at Chichester; at least, such has long been the tradition in the school.[2] On Jan. 19, 1733, he was admitted to Winchester College on the foundation, receiving his board, lodging, and tuition free.[3] At this famous school, in the venerable cathedral city of Winchester, Collins remained seven years. He was fortunate in having for schoolfellows several youths of more than ordinary abilities in literature. Foremost among them was his lifelong friend Joseph Warton, a respectable poet and critic, and for many years head-master of Winchester College. Other friends were William Whitehead, afterwards poet laureate, and James Hampton, the translator of Polybius.

At Winchester Collins made his first verses of which we have record. It is said that when twelve years old he wrote

Dallaway, London, 1815, vol. I, p. 186. Dallaway also mentions a Thomas Collins, sheriff of Sussex from 1663 to 1683; Henry Collins, who held the same office from 1702 to 1714; Roger Collins, incumbent of the Church of St. Olave, Chichester, for forty-five years, who died in 1707.

[1] From a list of the mayors on the walls of the council chamber at Chichester. The name of Thomas Collins occurs in 1631 and 1646 as well as in 1619.

[2] The Aldine *Collins*, London, 1894, p. x.

[3] " Gulielm. Collins de Chichester. Com. Sussex. Bapt. 1 Jan. 1721. Adm. 19 Jan. 1733."— Register of Winchester College.

a poem on a *Battle of the School Books*, one line of which was remembered long afterwards:

> And every Gradus flapped his leathern wing.[1]

In 1739 two short poems by him appeared in *The Gentleman's Magazine*.[2] A more unmistakable proof of his poetical powers was the *Persian Eclogues*, which Joseph Warton says were written at Winchester, when Collins was about seventeen years of age.

Of the poet's scholarship at this period there is no very certain evidence, but it seems probable that he was a brilliant student. Gilbert White (White of Selborne) recalled that he was "distinguished for his early proficiency, and his turn for elegant composition"; but White had not known Collins at Winchester, and was writing many years after his death. Johnson says that "his English exercises were better than his Latin"; but also that, in 1740, when Collins was ready for the university, "he stood first in the list of the scholars to be received in succession at New College," and the statement is confirmed by White, who adds that Joseph Warton stood second in the list.

On March 21, 1740, Collins was entered as a commoner on the books of Queen's College, Oxford, and the register of the university contains the record of his matriculation on the following day.[3] It is not known just when he went to

---

[1] *The European Magazine and London Review*, December, 1795, p. 377. The reminiscence is anonymous.

[2] In *The Gentleman's Magazine* for March, 1734, in the register of books published that month, is mentioned a poem on the royal nuptials, by a William Collins. The poem has never been found; it is doubtful if the subject of this sketch, then a schoolboy of thirteen, could have been the author.

[3] "17$\frac{39}{40}$ . . . William Collins Com^r—— Mar. 21."— Entrance Book of Queen's College. "17$\frac{39}{40}$ Mar. 22 Coll. Reg. Gul: Collins 18 Gul: Fil: de Chichester in Com: Sussexiæ. Gen: Fil."— Register of Matriculations of the University of Oxford.

Oxford to reside. He was disappointed in his hope of an election to New College (which is allied with Winchester College through their common founder), as there happened to be no vacancy at that time ; but on July 29, 1741, he was admitted a "demy" of Magdalen College,[1] through the influence, it is said, of his cousin William Payne, one of the fellows.[2] He received the degree of B. A. on Nov. 18, 1743.[3]

Our certain knowledge of the poet's university career goes little further than these external and meagre facts. But it is a probable surmise that his life at Oxford was a mixture of study, indolence, and dissipation. His poem *The Manners*[4] seems to hint at the dissipation, which is made the more probable by his temperament, his way of life in London soon after, and some of the reasons cited below for his leaving the university. His college friend White, however, declared that so long as he knew him Collins was "very temperate in his eating and drinking." The indolence so conspicuous in the poet's character when, as a poor author in London, he had every incentive to industry, could hardly have been absent in the leisure of academic days. In fact, Langhorne, his first editor, says that "during his residence at Queen's he was at once distinguished for genius and indolence ; his exercises, when he could be prevailed on to write, bearing the visible characteristics of both."[5] But in spite of indolence and dissipation Collins must have devoted considerable time to study. That he received his degree after the usual

---

[1] "Anno Domini 1741 . . . July 29 . . . in numerum Semicom. (vulgo dict : Demyes) admissi sunt Vernon . . . et Collins." — Register of Magdalen College.

[2] The Aldine *Collins*, London, 1894, p. xv.

[3] In the Register of the University, among B.A., "Term°. Sti Michælis 1743," is found "Gul. Collins e C. Magd.   Nov. 18."

[4] Lines 9–12.

[5] Langhorne's *Collins*, London, 1765, p. vi.

period of residence, and even aspired to a fellowship, means little, for scholarship at Oxford was then in a bad way; there were no examinations for degrees, and fellowships commonly went by favor, not by merit. But Johnson, who made Collins's acquaintance not long after, has borne testimony that he was "a man of extensive literature, . . . acquainted not only with the learned tongues, but with the Italian, French, and Spanish languages."

The only anecdote regarding the poet's life at the university is the following, narrated by White : "It happened one afternoon, at a tea visit, that several intelligent friends were assembled at his rooms to enjoy each other's conversation, when in comes a member of a certain college, as remarkable at that time for his brutal disposition as for his good scholarship ; who, though he met with a circle of the most peaceable people in the world, was determined to quarrel ; and, though no man said a word, lifted up his foot and kicked the tea-table, and all its contents, to the other side of the room. Our poet, though of a warm temper, was so confounded at the unexpected downfall, and so astonished at the unmerited insult, that he took no notice of the aggressor, but, getting up from his chair calmly, he began picking up the slices of bread and butter, and the fragments of his china, repeating very mildly,

Invenias etiam disjecti membra poetae."

It is not known just when Collins left the university. His poem addressed to Hanmer is dated "Oxford, Dec. 3, 1743"; he probably took up his residence in London soon after. Various reasons have been given for his leaving Oxford before the expiration of his demyship ; failure to get a fellowship, debts, and "a desire to partake of the dissipation and gaiety of London," are mentioned by Mr. Ragsdale, who made his acquaintance at about this time. The following words by

White throw some light upon the poet's life at the university as well as upon his reasons for leaving it: "As he brought with him, for so the whole turn of his conversation discovered, too high an opinion of his school acquisitions, and a sovereign contempt for all academic studies and discipline, he never looked with any complacency on his situation in the university, but was always complaining of the dullness of a college life. In short, he threw up his demyship, and, going to London, commenced a man of the town, spending his time in all the dissipation of Ranelagh, Vauxhall, and the playhouses."

The next five or six years, during which Collins resided in or near London,[1] were the great period of his life. In them he wrote nearly all his best poetry. During them he enjoyed the friendship of such men as Johnson, Garrick, and Thomson. And in these years, too, like so many other literary adventurers before and since, he suffered the distress of poverty and the bitterer pangs of disillusion and unmerited neglect.

Collins came to London with high hopes and gay spirits. The secluded life of the university lay behind him ; before him opened the world.[2] "He was romantic enough to suppose," says White, "that his superior abilities would draw the attention of the great world, by means of whom he was to make his fortune." Johnson adds that he had "many projects in his head and very little money in his pocket." He was soon to learn that the Muse was a poor paymistress. Meanwhile he was not wholly without the means of subsistence. Ragsdale says that the poet's uncle, Col. Edmund

---

[1] Of his lodging-places there is no record save the statement by White that "he lodged in a little house with a Miss Bundy, at the corner of King's Square Court, Soho, now a warehouse, for a long time together."

[2] See *The Manners*, 1–20, 75–78.

Martin, who had supported him at the university, continued his benefactions for a time in London, through a Mr. Payne, who had charge of the colonel's affairs. And the same friend, who evidently needed only a change of sex to make him a professional gossip, tells a story about the young adventurer which reminds one of Goldsmith and his happy willingness to scatter the money of his relatives:

"When Mr. William Collins came from the university, he called on his cousin Payne, gaily dressed and with a feather in his hat; at which his relation expressed surprise, and told him his appearance was by no means that of a young man who had not a single guinea he could call his own. This gave him great offence; but remembering his sole dependence for subsistence was in the power of Mr. Payne, he concealed his resentment; yet could not refrain from speaking freely behind his back, and saying he thought him a d——d dull fellow; though, indeed, this was an epithet he was pleased to bestow on every one who did not think as he would have them. His frequent demands for a supply obliged Mr. Payne to tell him he must pursue some other line of life, for he was sure Colonel Martin would be displeased with him for having done so much."

Somewhat later, apparently, Collins came into a little property of his own. Ten years before, in 1734,[1] his father had died in embarrassed circumstances.[2] But by the death of his mother, in July, 1744,[1] Collins inherited, with his two sisters, the property which had been secured by his mother's marriage settlement to her children.[3] The poet's share, however, seems to have been small, and was soon gone.

There is some evidence that at about this time, before Collins finally decided to give himself wholly to literature,

---

[1] From the family tablet in the Church of St. Andrew, Chichester.
[2] So Ragsdale says.
[3] The Aldine *Collins*, London, 1894, p. xvii.

he thought of entering the army or the church. It is said, but upon doubtful authority,[1] that he visited Colonel Martin, then with his regiment in Flanders, and that his uncle "found him too indolent even for the army." There is more reason to believe that Collins had all along been intended for the church;[2] and it is reported that after returning from Flanders he took steps toward obtaining a curacy.[3] If the poet had any intention of taking orders, it was soon abandoned, and he turned to literature for support.

Literature could be made to yield support, even in the middle of the eighteenth century, but not by a man like Collins, who had neither the popular gift of Pope nor the resolution of Johnson. " He designed many works," says the latter, " but his great fault was irresolution ; or the frequent calls of immediate necessity broke his scheme and suffered him to pursue no settled purpose. A man doubtful of his dinner, or trembling at a creditor, is not much disposed to abstracted meditation or remote inquiries. He published proposals for a *History of the Revival of Learning;* and I have heard him speak with great kindness of Leo the Tenth, and with keen resentment of his tasteless successor. But probably not a page of his history was ever written. He planned several tragedies, but he only planned them. He wrote now-and-then odes and other poems, and did something, however little."

There follows, in Johnson's life of the poet, an anecdote which, like the parallel story about Goldsmith, shows Johnson

---

[1] *History of Chichester,* by Alexander Hay, Chichester, 1804, p. 527. Fawkes and Woty's *Poetical Calendar* (December, 1763) and Langhorne place the visit later, shortly before Colonel Martin's death.

[2] " His father . . . intended him for the service of the church; and with this view . . . he was admitted a scholar of . . . Winchester College." — Langhorne's *Collins,* London, 1765, p. v.

[3] Hay's *Chichester,* Chichester, 1804, p. 527.

to us as the Mr. Greatheart of poor literary pilgrims in " the wilderness of this world."   " By degrees," says Johnson, " I gained his confidence ; and one day was admitted to him when he was immured by a bailiff, that was prowling in the street.   On this occasion recourse was had to the booksellers, who, on the credit of a translation of Aristotle's *Poeticks*, which he engaged to write with a large commentary, advanced as much money as enabled him to escape into the country. He showed me the guineas safe in his hand."   A recent French critic remarks upon the incident, with delicate humor, " C'est peut-être l'unique fois qu'Aristote ait rendu ce service à un lettré." [1]

In such untoward circumstances Collins composed the poems which have secured him lasting fame, although even these, if Ragsdale's statement can be trusted, were written for the purpose of getting money.   " To raise a present subsistence he set about writing his odes ; and, having a general invitation to my house, he frequently passed whole days there, which he employed in writing them, and as frequently burning what he had written, after reading them to me : many of them, which pleased me, I struggled to preserve, but without effect ; for, pretending he would alter them, he got them from me and thrust them into the fire."   The poet's literary fastidiousness is mentioned also by Thomas Warton, who says : " I have seen all his odes, already published, in his own handwriting ; they had the marks of repeated correction : he was perpetually changing his epithets."

Collins's earlier intention was to publish his odes jointly with those of his friend Joseph Warton.   This appears from a letter written by the latter to Thomas Warton, in which he says : " Collins met me in Surrey, at Guildford races, when I wrote out for him my odes, and he likewise communicated some of his to me ; and being both in very high spirits we

---

[1] Émile Montégut, *Heures de Lecture d'un Critique*, Paris, 1891, p. 183.

took courage, resolved to join our forces, and to publish them
immediately. . . . Collins is not to publish the odes unless
he gets ten guineas for them." [1]

The plan of joint publication was for some reason abandoned, and the poems of the two friends appeared separately
in December, 1746. Warton's little book went to a second
edition in the next year.[2] Collins's odes fell flat, and the
best efforts of his publisher could not work off the edition
of a thousand copies.[3] How great was the disappointment
of the proud and sensitive author we could easily imagine,
even if there had not come down to us the story that, "con-
ceiving a just indignation against a blind and tasteless age,"
he "burnt the remaining copies with his own hands."

But although the odes did not catch the popular ear, they
could hardly fail to raise the poet's reputation among men of
letters. In particular, Collins seems to have been intimate
with Thomson during the year and a half between the publication of the odes and Thomson's death. It is said that he
took lodgings at Richmond and entered that jovial circle of
friends some of whose portraits Thomson sketched in *The
Castle of Indolence.*[5] The memorial verses by Collins, pub-

---

[1] John Wooll's *Memoirs of J. Warton*, London, 1806, p. 14, foot-note.
The letter is undated. It cannot be earlier than May, 1745, for it refers to
the ode on the death of Colonel Ross, who fell at Fontenoy in that month ;
nor later than June, 1746, when the ode was published in Dodsley's
Museum.

[2] *Odes on Various Subjects*, by Joseph Warton, 2d ed., London, 1747.

[3] Langhorne's fling at the publisher as "a favourer of genius, *when
once it has made its way to fame*," brought out a reply in *The Monthly
Review* (vol. XXXII, p. 294) that "the bookseller actually purchased the
copy, at a very handsome price (for those times), and, at his own
expence and risk, did all in his power to introduce Mr. Collins to the
notice of the public." Langhorne removed the sentence in subsequent
editions.

[4] Langhorne's *Collins*, London, 1765, p. xi.

[5] The Aldine *Collins*, London, 1894, p. xxiii.

lished the year after Thomson's death, certainly bear the impress of personal love and grief.

The days of Collins's poverty were now drawing to a close. In April, 1749, Colonel Martin died,[1] and left to the poet about £2000, "a sum," says Johnson, "which Collins could scarcely think exhaustible, and which he did not live to exhaust." Soon afterwards he seems to have left London and taken up his residence in his native city.[2]

Of Collins's literary labors and plans in these days of newly acquired competence and ease there are several hints. His last poem which has been preserved, the *Ode on the Popular Superstitions of the Highlands of Scotland*, was occasioned by a friend's return to Scotland, toward the end of the year 1749, and evidently was composed at about that time. The following letter[3] is interesting both for its reference to another ode, which has never been discovered, and also because it is the only extant letter from the poet's hand. It refers to a musical performance of *The Passions*, and is addressed to Dr. William Hayes, Professor of Music in Oxford University.

" Sir,

" Mr. Blackstone, of Winchester, some time since informed me of the honour you had done me at Oxford last summer ; for which I return you my sincere thanks. I have another

---

[1] *The Gentleman's Magazine*, April, 1749, register of deaths.

[2] See Collins's letter, p. xxii and T. Warton's letter, p. xxiv.

[3] Printed in Seward's *Supplement to Anecdotes of Some Distinguished Persons*, London, 1797, p. 123, where it is preceded by this statement : " The following letter . . . to Dr. Hayes . . . was permitted to decorate this Collection, by the kindness of his son. . . . The music of the ode to which it refers was excellently well adapted to the words. The choruses were very full and majestic, and the airs gave completely the spirit of the Passions which they were intended to imitate."

more perfect copy of the Ode ; which, had I known your obliging design, I would have communicated to you.

"Inform me by a line, if you should think one of my better judgement acceptable. In such case I could send you one written on a nobler subject ; and which, tho' I have been persuaded to bring it forth in London, I think more calculated for an audience in the University. The subject is the Music of the Grecian Theatre ; in which I have, I hope naturally, introduced the various characters with which the chorus was concerned, as Œdipus, Medea, Electra, Orestes, etc., etc. The composition, too, is probably more correct, as I have chosen the ancient Tragedies for my models, and only copied the most affecting passages in them.

"In the mean time, you would greatly oblige me by sending the score of the last. If you can get it written, I will readily answer the expence. If you send it with a copy or two of the Ode (as printed at Oxford) to Mr. Clarke, at Winchester, he will forward it to me here.

"I am, Sir, with great respect,

"Your obliged humble servant,

"CHICHESTER, SUSSEX,   "WILLIAM COLLINS.
       "November 8, 1750.

"P. S. Mr. Clarke past some days here while Mr. Worgan was with me; from whose friendship, I hope, he will receive some advantage."

Other poems, of uncertain date, may for convenience be mentioned at this point. "He also shewed us," writes Thomas Warton, speaking of the year 1754, "another ode, of two or three four-lined stanzas, called *The Bell of Arragon;* on a tradition that, anciently, just before a king of Spain died, the great bell of the cathedral of Sarragossa, in Arragon, tolled spontaneously. It began thus :

> ' The bell of Arragon, they say,
> ' Spontaneous speaks the fatal day,' etc.

Soon afterwards were these lines :

> ' Whatever dark aërial power,
> ' Commission'd haunts the gloomy tower.'

The last stanza consisted of a moral transition to his own death and knell, which he called ' some simpler bell.' . . . Dr. Warton, my brother, has a few fragments of some other odes, but too loose and imperfect for publication, yet containing traces of high imagery."

Collins had not lost his talent for projects. In 1750 he proposed to Thomas Warton "a scheme of a review, to be called *The Clarendon Review*, and to be printed at the university press, under the conduct and authority of the university." When it is remembered that the reviews of the eighteenth century were booksellers' organs, written by literary hacks, Collins's idea is seen to be original and bold. It has since been realized, in substance, by the great independent reviews established in the first quarter of the present century ; in 1750 the project probably was not practicable. It appears, from references by Thomas Warton, that at this time Collins also resumed his purpose of writing a history of the Revival of Learning, and collected many scarce books to aid him in this labor.[1]

But now, in the midst of prosperity, and when he had hardly reached the maturity of his powers, there crept into the mind of the poet an insidious and terrible malady, which darkened all his remaining days and made him one of the most pitiable of men. Collins's disease was mental ; but its exact nature cannot be determined, as the reports concerning it are vague and sometimes conflicting. Apparently it developed slowly, and was always variable if not strictly intermittent.

[1] See p. xl.

Johnson says that "the approaches of this dreadful malady he began to feel soon after his uncle's death." Thomas Warton writes: "I often saw Collins in London in 1750. This was before his illness. . . . About Easter, the next year, I was in London; when, being given over, and supposed to be dying, he desired to see me, that he might take his last leave of me; but he grew better, and in the summer he sent me a letter on some private business, which I have now by me, dated Chichester, June 9, 1751, written in fine hand, and without the least symptom of a disordered or debilitated understanding." Johnson says further (and is confirmed by Ragsdale) that "these clouds which he perceived gathering on his intellects, he endeavored to disperse by travel, and passed into France; but found himself constrained to yield to his malady, and returned. He was for some time confined in a house of lunaticks." Ragsdale adds that the mad-house was in Chelsea, and was kept by one McDonald. How long the unfortunate man remained there is unknown; but by September, 1754, when the Wartons paid him a visit, he had been removed to Chichester, where he lived with his sister Anne, now married, in a house adjoining the cathedral cloisters.[1] Here he remained till his death.

In its earlier stages the poet's malady took the form rather of weakness and depression than of derangement. Johnson says that when he visited Collins at Islington, soon after his return from France, "there was then nothing of disorder discernible in his mind by any but himself; but he had withdrawn from study, and travelled with no other book than an English Testament, such as children carry to the school: when his friend took it into his hand, out of curi-

---

[1] The house formerly belonged to the cathedral, but after the Reformation it passed into lay hands. Its front door, curiously enough, is *in* the outer wall of the cloister.

osity to see what companion a man of letters had chosen, ' I have but one book,' said Collins, ' but that is the best.' " Johnson adds : " His disorder was no alienation of mind, but general laxity and feebleness, a deficiency rather of his vital than his intellectual powers. What he spoke wanted neither judgement nor spirit ; but a few minutes exhausted him, so that he was forced to rest upon the couch, till a short cessation restored his powers, and he was again able to talk with his former vigour." This agrees with Thomas Warton's statement of his condition in 1754 : " He came to Oxford for change of air and amusement, where he stayed a month ; I saw him frequently, but he was so weak and low that he could not bear conversation. Once he walked from his lodgings, opposite Christ Church, to Trinity College, but supported by his servant. The same year, in September, I and my brother visited him at Chichester. . . . The first day he was in high spirits at intervals, but exerted himself so much that he could not see us the second."

But it is evident that later Collins's condition became much worse, and that at times he was violently deranged. White says : " How he got down to Oxford, I do not know ; but I myself saw him under Merton wall, in a very affecting situation, struggling, and conveyed by force, in the arms of two or three men, towards the parish of St. Clement, in which was a house that took in such unhappy objects." [1] The following anecdote, told to Thomas Warton by the clergyman who buried Collins, shows that even to the last the poet's condition varied greatly : [2] " Walking in my vicarial garden one Sunday evening, during Collins's last illness,

---

[1] This distressing incident can hardly have occurred, as the editor of the Aldine *Collins* thinks, during the visit to Oxford in 1754, or Warton would have mentioned it.

[2] See also the first passage from T. Warton's *History of English Poetry*, on p. xl.

I heard a female (the servant, I suppose) reading the Bible in his chamber. Mr. Collins had been accustomed to rave much, and make great moanings ; but while she was reading, or rather attempting to read, he was not only silent but attentive likewise, correcting her mistakes, which indeed were very frequent, through the whole of the twenty-seventh chapter of Genesis."

A modern specialist on insanity[1] gives the following opinion as to the nature of Collins's malady : " He was evidently an unpractical, visionary genius, wanting in stability of character and serious purpose, yet with a fine-grained nature, sensitive, and keenly appreciative of the beauty of truth. The causes of his mental derangement may be found, without doubt, in these congenital characteristics, in the stress of poverty and worry, and perhaps in his dissipation and intemperance. In general, the testimony points less to a disorder of his intellectual faculties than to a disturbance of his emotional nature. While the picture does not fall readily under any of the well-defined forms of insanity, it appears to conform most closely to the type called melancholia, and to that form of melancholia characterized by periods of great mental pain and wild agitation, with more composed intervals in which the patient exhibits much self-control and mental clearness. It is probable that the poet's debilitated physical condition during his last years was due to his mental disease."

In this pitiable state Collins lingered until June 12, 1759,[2] when he died in his sister's arms.[3] Three days later he was buried in the parish of St. Andrew.[4]

[1] See *Preface.*

[2] From a tablet erected by his sister in the Church of St. Andrew.

[3] *The Gentleman's Magazine*, November, 1789, in a notice of his sister's death.

[4] In the parish register, among the burials in the year 1759, is the entry : " June 15, William Collins, Gent." Mitford (in Dyce's *Collins*)

Collins was never married, and there is no certain evidence that he was ever in love. There is a tradition, however, that he loved a lady who did not return his passion. It is also said that she was his elder by a day, and that he wittily remarked, with a reference to his unhappy love-suit, that he came into the world "a day after the fair."[1] It has been surmised that the lady was the Miss Elizabeth Goddard to whom the ode on the death of Colonel Ross was addressed.[2]

No likeness of Collins has been preserved except the well-known portrait painted in his fourteenth year.[3] In Flaxman's bas-relief of the poet, on the tablet erected in Chichester Cathedral a generation after his death, the face is of the same general type;[4] but it is not known what originals the sculptor had, or whether a likeness was even attempted.[5] Johnson says of Collins that "his appearance was decent and manly." White's statement is more definite : "He was of moderate stature, of a light and clear complexion, with grey eyes, so very weak at times as hardly to bear a candle in the room, and often raising within him apprehensions of blindness." Langhorne's description is in two particulars at variance with White's : "Mr. Collins was, in stature, somewhat above the middle size; of a 'brown' [*i.e.*, dark] com-

---

says : "Collins is buried under the pew in the church [of St. Andrew], belonging to the house ; a stone tablet on the wall above." The tablet, however, which also records the death of several other members of the family, does not say that the poet is buried beneath.

[1] Seward's *Supplement to Anecdotes of Some Distinguished Persons*, London, 1797, p. 125. In *The European Magazine*, October, 1795, another version of the anecdote is given, according to which the occasion of the pun was his coming into a town the day after the lady had left it.

[2] See p. 109, and the variant reading of l. 37 in the *Ode to a Lady*.

[3] See the frontispiece in the Aldine *Collins*.

[4] See frontispiece.   [5] See p. xxxiii.

plexion, keen, expressive eyes, and a fixed, sedate aspect, which from intense thinking had contracted an habitual frown." [1]

Collins's personality in its main outlines is apparent from the foregoing sketch of his life. A few details may be added from the statements of his friends. White wrote of him that " he was passionately fond of music, good-natured and affable, warm in his friendships, and visionary in his pursuits." Ragsdale reports that " he was an acceptable companion everywhere "; that he was accustomed to make " diverting observations on the vanity and false consequence " of the " geniuses " who frequented the coffee-houses, and that " his manner of relating them to his particular friends was extremely entertaining." Johnson says that Collins's " knowledge [was] considerable, his views extensive, his conversation elegant, and his disposition chearful." He has faithfully recorded that in the first stages of the malady which clouded his closing years Collins " eagerly snatched that temporary relief with which the table and the bottle flatter and seduce." Johnson's summary of the poet's moral character deserves reprinting once more, in spite of its formality. The manifest struggle in it between fidelity to truth and tenderness for the memory of a dear friend reveals Johnson as well as Collins, and increases our confidence in the accuracy of the portrait, so far as Johnson could understand a man like Collins :

" His morals were pure, and his opinions pious ; in a long continuance of poverty and long habits of dissipation, it cannot be expected that any character should be exactly uniform. There is a degree of want by which the freedom of agency is almost destroyed ; and long association with fortuitous

---

[1] Langhorne makes no mention of having seen Collins ; but he was writing within six years after the poet's death, and had many literary friends in London, some of whom very likely had known Collins. White's description was written twenty-two years after Collins's death.

companions will at last relax the strictness of truth, and abate the fervour of sincerity. That this man, wise and virtuous as he was, passed always unentangled through the snares of life, it would be prejudice and temerity to affirm; but it may be said that at least he preserved the source of action unpolluted, that his principles were never shaken, that his distinctions of right and wrong were never confounded, and that his faults had nothing of malignity or design, but proceeded from some unexpected pressure or casual temptation."

It is evident that Collins was a good deal of a puzzle to Johnson. The latter saw the contradictions in his friend's nature, but could not understand them; and, truly, in his statement of them the contradictions seem irreconcilable. In particular, the hint that Collins was sometimes lacking in truth and sincerity is inconsistent with Johnson's warm admiration for his character as a whole. The attempt to lay the blame upon bad company is more charitable than penetrating. We may be sure that a more subtle interpreter would have seen more unity in the poet's sensitive, imaginative nature, and would have found the key to passages in his life which the sturdy Moralist could only wonder at and excuse. But on the main question we may take Johnson's word with absolute confidence. Samuel Johnson had an instinct for the genuine; and he accepted Collins, with all his mystery and contradictions, as a lovable and true man.[1]

[1] The following statement is worth reprinting, for the light it throws upon the poet's nature, although it may be unjust to his sister. The editor of the Aldine *Collins* says that the sister's will affords evidence that she separated from Dr. Durnford, her second husband, and her step-son's testimony as to her character must, therefore, be regarded with suspicion. "The Rev. Mr. Durnford, who resided at Chichester, and was the son of Dr. D., informed me in August, 1795, that the sister of Collins loved money to excess, and evinced so outrageous an aversion to her brother, because he squandered or gave away to the boys in the

II. THE ALLEGED NEGLECT OF COLLINS IN THE EIGHTEENTH CENTURY.

It is the common impression that the poetry of Collins was not appreciated in his own day, and that it lay neglected and almost unknown for nearly half a century after his death. While this impression has some foundation, it is far from being the precise truth. For one thing, it fails to distinguish between appreciation and popularity. Collins's poetry was not popular in the last century. It cannot strictly be said to be popular in the present century; but it has acquired what may be called a popularity at second hand: it has taken its place amid standard poetry, Collins's name is coupled with Gray's, and people feel that they ought to know about him whether they do know or not. This sort of reflected fame, of course, did not come to Collins at once, although its beginnings may be found a good while before the end of the last century.

In the matter of appreciation by a chosen few, in distinction from popularity, the main difference between the earlier and the later view is that Collins's critics in the eighteenth century did not realize the significance of his work in the historical development of English literature. They saw many of the beauties of his poems considered as isolated works of art ; but they did not see, and could hardly be expected to see, that he represented a transition between the old school

cloisters whatever money he had, that she destroyed, in a paroxysm of resentment, all his papers, and whatever remained of his enthusiasm for poetry, as far as she could. Mr. Hayley told me, when I visited him at Eartham, that he had obtained from her a small drawing by Collins; but it possessed no other value than as a memorial that the bard had attempted to handle the pencil as well as the pen." — MS. note by T. Park, Esq., in his copy of Collins's poems, afterwards in the possession of Mr. Mitford ; quoted in Dyce's *Collins*, p. *39.

of poetry and a new. It was the triumph of Romanticism in English literature at the beginning of the nineteenth century which brought Collins into new prominence, and established his fame on a broader basis. It is also true that the romantic elements in his poetry were those least relished at first. But there is abundant proof that Collins was appreciated fairly well, on the whole, by the more intelligent readers in his own century. The very references to him as "neglected" prove that the judicious, at least, already knew his worth, and that he had missed rather of popularity than of appreciation. In particular it appears that relatively too much has usually been made of Johnson's obtuse critique, and of Cowper's ignorance, until late in life, that there was such a poet as William Collins.

The evidence from the successive reprints of the poems may be found in detail in the *Bibliography*.[1] It is clear that there was, almost from the first, a considerable demand for the *Eclogues*, and after a few years a steady though moderate demand for the *Odes*. It is also clear that some time before the close of the century Collins had already taken his position among the standard English poets, although he was not yet sufficiently distinguished from the Wartons and Whiteheads and other small fry.

Analogous evidence is that furnished by the musical performance of certain of the *Odes*. Reference has already been made to the performance at Oxford, during the poet's lifetime, of *The Passions*. The present editor has recently discovered that the *Ode to Evening* was also set to music, and performed in London in 1785. In the British Museum is a manuscript of the words and music[2] with the following note: "Performed for the first time at The Academy of Ancient Music, Free Masons Hall, Great Queen St., Lincolns

---

[1] See *Appendix, C.*
[2] Add. MSS. 27636, f. 59.

Inn, April 14, 1785. (By request of Mr. Butler.) I. W. Call-
cott." The manuscript consists of twenty-six pages. A list
of instruments is given, showing that sixteen were used,
besides an organ. The latter was played by Dr. Cooke,
the organist of Westminster Abbey; the first violinist was
the famous Luigi Borghi; and of the thirteen singers four
were well known in their day. Altogether it was a distinguished company. At the end of the score is the entry," 23
minutes long. March 29, 1785." [1]

Another class of evidence consists of biographical sketches
and other memorials of the poet. These are scanty; but a
partial explanation may be found in the fact that on account
of Collins's mental disease and his secluded life he was
practically an exile from the great world for several years
before he died. His death, in 1759, apparently was not
recorded, at the time, in any publication. *The Biographical
Dictionary*, published in London in 1761, in twelve volumes,
contained no mention of him. The earliest biographical
sketch of Collins seems to have appeared in *The Poetical
Calendar* for December, 1763. This stated most of the facts
with some accuracy, although giving 1756 as the year of
his death, and concluded with a sketch of his character by
Johnson. It was reprinted in *The Gentleman's Magazine* for
January, 1764. Langhorne's edition of Collins, in 1765,
contained a short memoir of the poet. Johnson's life
of Collins (including the character-sketch already printed)
appeared in 1779 as a preface to Collins's poems in *The
English Poets*. Finally, in 1789, the poet obtained honorable
sepulture in the *Biographia Britannica* in an article of several
pages, made up chiefly from Langhorne and Johnson, with
long critical eulogies from *The Monthly Review*.

The dust of the poet had now long lain in his native city

---

[1] In fairness it should be added that Joseph Warton's *Ode to Fancy*,
set to music, is in the same volume.

without local memorial save for a line on the family tablet in St. Andrew's Church. But in 1789 steps were taken for the erection of a monument to him. In *The Gentleman's Magazine* for December of that year is a letter from Chichester, signed " W. G.," announcing the project and inquiring for portraits of " the venerable poet." [1] The same magazine, in September, 1795, contains a statement that the monument has been erected by " public subscription "; Flaxman's bas-relief is described, and the epitaph follows.[1] The latter has four lines which are especially significant for their bearing on the question at issue :

> Strangers to him, enamoured of his lays,
> This fond memorial of his talents raise ;
> For this the ashes of a bard require,
> Who touched the tenderest notes of pity's lyre.

The critical notices of Collins's poetry during the second half of the last century are more numerous, and often more enthusiastic, than is commonly supposed.[2]

The earliest known estimate of the *Odes* is from the hand of Gray. In a letter written a few days after the *Odes* appeared, he speaks of the author as having " a fine fancy, modelled upon the antique, a bad ear, great variety of words and images, with no choice at all." In view of Gray's fastidious coldness of temperament, this is no mean praise. His opinion that both Collins and Joseph Warton " deserve to last some years, but will not," is censure of the public taste, not of the poetry.

Shortly before the death of Collins, Goldsmith wrote of him : " The neglected author of the *Persian Eclogues*, which, however inaccurate, excel any in our language, is still alive ; happy, if insensible of our neglect, not raging at our ingrati-

---

[1] See *Appendix, B.*

[2] See *Appendix, B,* for more extended quotations from several of these notices.

tude." [1] The reference does more credit to the writer's heart than to his knowledge of Collins's poetry ; but it shows a feeling on Goldsmith's part, and doubtless on that of his literary set in London, that the poet then living in pitiful seclusion at Chichester had been a spirit of no common sort.[2]

The Monthly Review, a leading magazine of the time, reviewed the second edition of the *Eclogues* in 1757, and the *Odes* in 1764 upon their republication, not long before, in *The Poetical Calendar.* Whatever other strictures might be made upon these critical performances, they cannot be charged with lack of warmth. In the earlier notice the *Eclogues* are called " beautiful " and are highly praised in detail. Collins is referred to as " the too much neglected author " of the *Odes ;* and these are credited with " elegance " and " picturesque genius." In the later notice Collins is said to have " a luxuriance of imagination, a wild sublimity of fancy, and a felicity of expression so extraordinary that it might be supposed to be suggested by some superior power." If this is not criticism, at least it is rapture. The reviewer goes on to say that Collins " will indisputably bear away the palm from all his competitors " in lyric poetry, and that he " was too great to be popular." This within five years after the poet's early death.

The next year, Collins found his first editor in the person of Rev. Dr. Langhorne, himself a poet of some grace. The worth of the reverend gentleman's praise is considerably damaged by the abundance of it ; occasionally, however, as in the following sentence, he says something which is discriminative and shows real appreciation : " Milton was noto-

---

[1] *Enquiry into the Present State of Polite Learning in Europe,* London, 1774, p. 107. (The first edition appeared in April, 1759.)

[2] Cf. Johnson's letter to J. Warton, April 15, 1756 : " What becomes of poor dear Collins ? . . . That man is no common loss."

riously fond of high romance, and Gothic diableries, and Collins, who in genius and enthusiasm bore no very distant resemblance to Milton, was wholly carried away by the same attachments."

Johnson's criticism of his friend's poetry is painfully familiar to lovers of Collins. But the bits of praise half hidden amid the censure have not always received the attention they merit. Johnson did not use words carelessly; and he meant all that he said when he wrote that Collins's poems " are the productions of a mind not deficient in fire, nor unfurnished with knowledge either of books or life," and that his efforts " produced in happier moments sublimity and splendor." As to the gross misjudgment in the critique as a whole, every one knows that it resulted from limitations in Johnson's personality and point of view. But it has not always been known or remembered that, at the time when the *Lives of the Poets* came out, Johnson by no means represented all England in matters of literary taste. The rising tide of Romanticism was submerging old landmarks ; and even those critics who, like the Literary Dictator, still stood for the older tradition did not always endorse his judgment in particular cases. It is easy, therefore, to over-estimate the historical significance of his condemnation of Collins's poetry ; and this has commonly been done.

A different phase of the matter is brought forward by Mr. Dyce. He says : " In a manuscript letter by Beattie, in my possession, written immediately after the publication of the *Lives*, mention is made of the severity with which Milton, Gray, and even Littleton are handled by Johnson, but no notice is taken of the treatment of Collins." Mr. Dyce draws the inference that " Collins was an author so little known, that few readers were aware of the injustice of the doctor's criticism on his poetry." [1] The reasoning is

[1] Dyce's *Collins*, p. 33.

far from conclusive. Beattie may not have read the strictures on Collins at the time of writing, or there may have
been other reasons. This negative sort of evidence is at
best unsatisfactory, particularly when it is limited to the
silence of one man in one letter. If the silence had been
universal, the argument would be strong ; but it was not
universal. Whether or not Beattie knew the injustice of
Johnson's criticism on Collins, there were those who knew
it and protested against it. In *The Gentleman's Magazine*
for January, 1782, appeared two letters, signed " Philo-
Lyrister" and " H.," defending Collins with much warmth.
Philo-Lyrister says : " I own that I felt myself hurt by the
liberties which he [Johnson] has taken with two of our
most celebrated lyric poets, viz., Gray and Collins. . . . Let
Dr. Johnson, with all his erudition, produce me another
lyric ode equal to Collins's on the Passions ; indeed the
frequent public recitals of this last-mentioned poem are
a mark of its universally acknowledged excellence." The
letter is the more significant because the writer professes
to be an admirer of Johnson in general ; while its very
commonplaceness adds to its value as testimony upon the
point in hand, by showing that Collins's fame was already
spreading beyond the circle of the literary elect.

The letter by " H." is so appreciative, discriminating,
and scholarly that the part about Collins deserves reprinting
nearly in full: "In the *Elegy*, so generally thought original,
he [Gray] has borrowed much from a contemporary poet ;
whoever compares it with Collins's *Ode to Evening* will find
such marks of particular imitation as are of more importance
than all those with which Gray ornamented the bottom of
his pages. . . . That exquisite stanza which once concluded
the *Elegy* . . . is still more immediately borrowed from
Collins than any of the rest ; the original passage is in
the *Dirge in Cymbeline*. . . . Collins has had the misfortune

not to please Dr. J. [Johnson]. His works also are encumbered with a mass of absurd criticisms, written by his editor Langhorne, only to piece out a volume, and his four eclogues are mere trash ; yet a part of his odes will, notwithstanding, command the admiration of mankind, as long as poetical genius or poetical taste shall remain in the world."

These two letters, appearing in one magazine in the same month, and called forth by an admiration for Collins's poetry which would not allow Johnson's harsh verdict to go unchallenged, must represent like sentiments held by many readers of the *Eclogues* and the *Odes.* They far outweigh the negative evidence from Beattie's silence. The case is different, however, with Cowper's reference to Collins in a letter to Newton, on March 19, 1784. His words are : " A poet of no great fame, — of whom I did not know that he existed till I found him there [in Johnson's *Lives*]. . . . His name was Collins." But it should be remembered that Cowper's circumstances were exceptional. His early years, it is true, had been spent in the world ; but at that time Collins was little known. Cowper's madness, and the morbid religiousness which followed, transformed the elegant trifler of the Inner Temple into a pious recluse. In the atmosphere of strong theology and weak tea in which Cowper henceforth passed his days, he was not likely to make the acquaintance of a semi-pagan poet of limited popularity. In fact when Cowper did hear of Collins at last, his interest in him was not literary but religious.[1]

---

[1] " I have lately finished eight volumes of Johnson's *Prefaces*, or *Lives of the Poets.* In all that ‚number I observe but one man, — a poet of no great fame, — of whom I did not know that he existed till I found him there, whose mind seems to have had the slightest tincture of religion ; and he was hardly in his senses. His name was Collins." — Cowper's *Works*, London, 1836, vol. V, p. 11.

In short, as Johnson did not fully represent the literary taste of England in the last quarter of the century, so Cowper, by reason of peculiar circumstances, did not fully represent its literary knowledge.[1] As additional proof of this may be mentioned the fact that in the next year a writer in *The European Magazine*, speaks of Collins as "the favoured child of poesy, whose productions in every line bear the most indubitable stamp of that divine enthusiasm which characterizes genius."[2] Of like purport is the honor paid to the *Oriental Eclogues*, in 1785, by an entire essay being devoted to them in a volume of critical essays by an acute critic of the day, where they have for fellows *Cooper's Hill, Lycidas, Windsor Forest, Grongar Hill, Ruins of Rome, Elegy Written in a Country Churchyard, The Deserted Village,* and *The Seasons.* Nor were they placed amid this distinguished company to be disgraced by contrast, the critic finally pronouncing that "the *Eclogues,* with all the faults that have been pointed out, have such poetical merit that . . . they have nothing to fear from a comparison with any of their predecessors."[3]

It is not necessary to trace the history of the growth of Collins's fame to the very limit of the century. The record may appropriately close with a short extract from the preface to his works in *The Poets of Great Britain*, edited by Robert Anderson, in 1794: "His odes . . . rank among the first lyric performances in the English language. . . . They

---

[1] In fact he did not fully represent the literary knowledge of the educated class, at least, even in far-away New England. Nine years before Cowper confessed his ignorance, Mrs. John Adams, writing to her husband three days after the battle of Bunker Hill, says : "Those favorite lines of Collins continually sound in my ears : —

'How sleep the brave,' etc."

[2] *The European Magazine*, August, 1785. The letter is signed "X."

[3] *Critical Essays*, by John Scott, London, 1785, p. 184.

entitle Collins to an indisputable preëminence above all his competitors in that province of poetry, except Dryden and Gray." [1]

III. COLLINS AND ROMANTICISM.

Collins's fame was slow in coming, partly because he outran the literary taste of his age. He was a pioneer in Romanticism, and the public and the critics were not yet ready for Romanticism. Collins was a romanticist by nature, in temperament and type of mind ranging rather with Shelley and Keats than with Addison, Pope, or Johnson. But he was not wholly a romanticist ; elements of a true Classicism were deep within him. And he fell upon times in which a pseudo-classical ideal predominated. The history of his poetic development is the resultant of the three forces indicated, of which the last rapidly declined, and the second remained about stationary, while the first steadily increased.

If Collins had not written a line, we should still have known that he sympathized deeply with the new movement which was beginning to transform literature in England. One evidence of this is the attitude of his friend Joseph Warton, who in the preface to his own odes affirmed the conviction that "the fashion of moralizing in verse has been carried too far," and that "invention and imagination" are "the chief faculties of a poet." [2] When it is remembered

[1] *A Complete Edition of the Poets of Great Britain*, Edinburgh, 1794, vol. IX, p. 515.

[2] "The public has been so much accustomed of late to didactic poetry alone, and essays on moral subjects, that any work where the imagination is much indulged will perhaps not be relished or regarded. The author therefore of these pieces is in some pain lest certain austere critics should think them too fanciful and descriptive. But as he is convinced that the fashion of moralizing in verse has been carried too far, and as he looks upon invention and imagination to be the chief faculties of a poet, so he will be happy if the following odes may be looked

how intimate the two men were, and that their first intention had been to publish their odes jointly, we may fairly assume that the preface expressed the views of Collins as well.

From Thomas Warton we learn that Collins was fond of black-letter reading and had collected many rare old books illustrating the earlier periods of English literature.[1]

upon as an attempt to bring back poetry into its right channel." — *Odes on Several Subjects*, by Joseph Warton, London, 1746.

[1] "My lamented friend Mr. William Collins, whose odes will be remembered while any taste for true poetry remains, shewed me this piece [Skelton's *Nigramansir*] at Chichester, not many months before his death; and pointed it out as a very rare and valuable curiosity. He intended to write the history of the Restoration of Learning under Leo the Tenth, and with a view to that design had collected many scarce books." — *The History of English Poetry*, by T. Warton, section XXXIII, foot-note.

"In the dispersed library of the late Mr. William Collins, I saw a thin folio of two sheets in black letter, containing a poem in the octave stanza, entitled, *Fabyl's Ghoste*, printed by John Rastell in the year 1533." — *Ibid.*, section XLI.

"Among the books of my friend the late Mr. William Collins of Chichester, now dispersed, was a collection of short comic stories in prose, printed in the black letter under the year 1570." — *Ibid.*, section LII.

"I was informed by the late Mr. Collins of Chichester, that Shakespeare's *Tempest*, for which no origin is yet assigned, was formed on this favorite romance [*Aurelio and Isabella*]. But although this information has not proved true on examination, an useful conclusion may be drawn from it, that Shakespeare's story is somewhere to be found in an Italian novel, at least that the story preceded Shakespeare. Mr. Collins had searched this subject with no less fidelity than judgment and industry: but his memory failing in his last calamitous indisposition, he probably gave me the name of one novel for another." — *Ibid.*, section LX.

Of like purport, as showing Collins's knowledge of the Elizabethan drama, is the following: "That our poet admired Ben Jonson, we learn from Tom Davies [bookseller and would-be actor], who, speaking of the epilogue to *Every Man Out of His Humour*, at the presentation before Queen Elizabeth, observes, 'Mr. Collins, the author of several justly esteemed poems, first pointed out to me the particular beauties of

His enthusiasm for the Renaissance, and his long-cherished plan of writing a history of the Revival of Learning, also indicate his sympathy with the earlier Romanticism. And, finally, Johnson's half-mournful description of his friend's romantic tendencies shows that this man, born when Pope was in the heyday of his power, and dying when Johnson ruled literary London with a bludgeon of common sense, was yet brother to Spenser, to the youthful Milton, to Chatterton and Blake, to the many ill-regulated enthusiasts and poetic dreamers of the early nineteenth century.[1]

When we turn to the poems themselves, we see in them an interesting struggle between Collins's natural romantic tendencies, his natural classic tendencies, and the literary conventions of the day.

The early minor poems all show, in varying degrees, the lyric instinct which had become so rare amid the prevailing didacticism in English verse. In the songs about Fidele and Damon the romantic elements of love, nature, and the supernatural are handled with simplicity and truth ; while the introduction of folklore in the former is a prophecy of the *Ode to Fear* and the *Ode on the Popular Superstitions of the Highlands.* The obvious elements of conventionalism in these slight poems do not call for special remark.

In the *Oriental Eclogues* the struggle between conventional

this occasional address.'" (*Dramatic Miscellanies*, vol. II, p. 77.) — Dyce's *Collins*, p. 12.

[1] " He had employed his mind chiefly on the works of fiction, and subjects of fancy ; and, by indulging some peculiar habits of thought, was eminently delighted with those flights of imagination which pass the bounds of nature, and to which the mind is reconciled only by a passive acquiescence in popular traditions. He loved fairies, genii, giants, and monsters ; he delighted to rove through the meanders of enchantment, to gaze on the magnificence of golden palaces, to repose by the waterfalls of Elysian gardens." — *Lives of the Poets*, London, 1820, vol. XI, p. 268.

form and new subject-matter is patent. The artificial pastoral was not yet quite dead in England ; it had been kept alive by the mighty names of Vergil, Spenser, and Milton, and recently by the example of Pope. It was, therefore, natural enough that the youthful Collins should write pastorals. What is noteworthy is that he sought for new metal to pour into the time-worn moulds, and anticipated Southey, Byron, and Moore in turning to the Orient for poetic material. The result, it must be admitted, is tame ; but the mildness of the romantic flavor is easily explained. Salmon's *History of Persia*, from which Collins got his inspiration, although sensible and mildly interesting, is not imaginative or picturesque ; and Collins showed that he was greatly athirst by sucking from it as much romance as he did. But even if the poet had had a richer treasury, he would not have dared to display its stores more freely. The apologetic tone of the preface is significant. Collins was evidently afraid that the "rich and figurative style" and the "elegancy and wildness of thought" might offend the taste of his readers. Romanticism was yet a timid thing in England.[1] Modern readers find the *Oriental Eclogues* less wild than wooden ; for there is much that is conventional, not only in the style and verse, but even in the subject-matter and spirit. A didactic motive is apparent throughout, as in the handling of similar material by Addison and Johnson. The truism that virtue is essential to lasting love and happiness, and the hackneyed themes of pastoral love and rural delights, constitute the warp and woof of the first and third eclogues, and enter largely into the texture of the other two. Oriental love, which was to receive such sensuous treatment later at the hands of Byron and Moore, is kept within the bounds of a decent tameness.

[1] See W. L. Phelps's *Beginnings of the English Romantic Movement*, passim.

Even the fact of polygamy is politely ignored. Only one Zara weeps for the distant Hassan ; and Abbas, the Persian monarch, might have been an English gentleman except for a little initial despotism in his manner of appropriating the rustic Abra. The fine opportunities for pictorial effect in the second eclogue are imperfectly developed, although the local coloring here is the best in the series ; the novel situation in the desert is made subordinate to shallow moralizing, current at the time, about the evils of " trade." Similarly, in the fourth eclogue, the scenic possibilities of midnight in devastated Circassia are largely sacrificed to commonplaces of pastoral description. In brief, the *Oriental Eclogues* are significant in the history of English Romanticism rather for their tendencies than for their achievement.

In the *Epistle Addressed to Sir Thomas Hanmer* the occasion overrode the poet. The result was the least individual of Collins's poems. The epistolary form, the conventional metre and style, the gross flattery, the half-blind estimate of Shakspere, — in all these Collins was hardly more than an amanuensis for the spirit of the age. Yet even in this poem may be detected some signs of the individuality of the man who was soon to write the *Odes Descriptive and Allegorical*. The references to Greek literature and the Renaissance are significant. The allusions to Shakspere's idyllic plays and to the fairyland of *A Midsummer-Night's Dream* and *The Tempest* remind one of the *Song from Shakespear's Cymbeline* and of the delicate Arcadian fancy in several of the odes. And the instinct for the sculpturesque and picturesque, soon to be revealed in the *Odes*, is suggested here also by the wish that painters would go to Shakspere for subjects and by the vivid sketches of two great scenes from the plays.

In the *Odes* of 1747 we pass into a new atmosphere. Here the influence of convention sinks to a subordinate place, and classic and romantic tendencies become dominant. The literary fashions of the day linger here and there in diction and phrasing, in an occasional frigid personification, and in the literary or political didacticism which underlies several of the odes; but over these matters we need not linger. The classic and the romantic elements require more detailed examination. We will begin with the latter.

In these odes Collins reveals his poetical creed by his literary allusions. Spenser and his school, Shakspere, Milton, Otway — that belated Elizabethan, — these are the gods of his idolatry among English poets ; while he speaks slightingly of the then popular Waller, and implies that pathos is a lost note in the British lyre. His practice conforms to his theory. The *Odes*, in their main effect, are not intellectual and didactic, but imaginative, pictorial, and lyrical. They are not chiefly to be thought out, but to be looked at, felt, and sung. The versification is an index to the spirit of the whole. The end-stopped pentameter couplet of the *Eclogues* and the *Epistle*, a form so admirable for narration, exposition, or satire, so ill-adapted for lyric flow, has given place to a variety of measures that fitly embody the subject-matter.

But it is the subject-matter itself which most clearly shows the poet's trend toward Romanticism. Collins was, literally, a visionary. He saw visions. He lived in a world of imaginary beings, some beautiful, some terrible, some the creation of folklore and legend, and some the product of his own imagination. If the *Odes* be read rapidly, with this single point in view, it is surprising how constantly the poet's thought escapes from reality to an imaginary world. Even *The Manners*, in praise of the observation of the real world, is all compact of fancies about " wizard Passions," " giant Follies," and " magic shores." *The Passions* is didactic in intent, praising the simplicity of Greek music above the complex music of modern times.

But the lesson is a picture. And in place of the historical Alexander in Dryden's similar ode, Collins painted a new Pandemonium and Elysium in one, where bedlam Passions mingle with the Loves and Graces. The political and military events of the day, passing through this poet's mind, are transformed into a dream-land peculiarly his own, where ideal figures stand out in colossal bas-relief, as in the *Ode to Mercy*, or, as in the *Ode to a Lady* and *How Sleep the Brave*, shadowy forms at once delicate and majestic mourn over the graves of the heroic dead.

But the *Ode to Fear*, the *Ode to Liberty*, and the *Ode on the Poetical Character* are richest in elements of the supernatural or semi-supernatural. In the beginning of the last-named, Collins's imagination manifestly revels in the marvellous legend of the magic girdle; he is wandering amid the mazes of *The Faerie Queene*. The description of creation, an echo from the idealism of Plato and Spenser, beats with an inward heat, an intense pleasure in the fantastic richness of the picture. And the ideal landscape with which the ode ends had its inspiration in a reverence, amounting almost to worship, for Milton as the poet of the supernatural sublime. The antistrophe of the *Ode to Liberty* shows how well Collins knew the poetic value of old legends and traditions; the fabled disruption of Britain from the mainland is thoroughly romantic in its rugged wildness and a certain element of the monstrous; while the second epode is rich with imaginative beauty deriving from old Celtic sources. The *Ode to Fear* marks the climax of the supernatural element in these *Odes* of 1747. A true imaginative shudder runs through the whole. It is conceived and expressed throughout with a vigor which shows that the poet had himself lifted " the veil between " and was looking out with pleasurable awe into the dim, vast realm of imaginative Terror and the dark Sublime. From the classic drama he selects those aspects which are most closely allied to the murkiness of the "Gothic" mind ; and the conception, in the strophe, of fiends who " over Nature's wrecks and wounds preside " is essentially Teutonic, the counterpart of the Greek belief in fair spirits, the guardian divinities of mountains, trees, and running brooks.

The treatment of nature in the *Odes* is not remarkable except in the *Ode to Evening*. A French critic has recently observed that in this poem Collins anticipated the work of the modern " impressionist " school ; and he points out that " the phenomena of evening, which dissolve progressively all natural form and destroy the solidity of every object," are peculiarly adapted for treatment in accordance with the doctrine of the impressionists that " things are more poetic by their aspects than by their forms, and by their colors than by their substance." [1]

But curious as this anticipation is, it concerns us more just now to ask what relation the poem bore to Collins's own environment and to the rest of his work. It must have had a close relation, although it seems so unique. It cannot have been a literary freak, a poem-child of the nineteenth century born out of due time.

What view of the matter did Collins himself probably take ? It is not likely that he supposed he was doing anything unusual. And in a way he was not. It is singular

---

[1] "*L'Ode au Soir* est en effet de la poésie impressioniste au premier chef ; d'instinct, Collins a découvert et appliqué inconsciemment la théorie que l'on sait, et il lui a suffi pour cela du désir d'imiter son objet aussi étroitement que possible, car s'il est vrai que les choses sont plus poétiques par leurs aspects que par leurs formes et par leurs couleurs que par leur substance, on comprendra aisément comment le phénomène du soir, qui dissout progressivement toute forme naturelle et détruit la solidité de toute objet, s'accommode mieux que tout autre d'être traité selon cette doctrine, qui, si elle est douteuse dans d'autres cas, est absolument vraie dans celui-là." — *Heures de Lecture d'un Critique,* by Émile Montégut, Paris, 1891, pp. 213, 214.

that this poem, in the last stanza, is marred by worse conventionalism than can be found elsewhere in the *Odes.* Furthermore, the mood of the poem is common enough. Eventide, when all things are idealized by dimness and calm, is Nature's popular poetry, felt by the most callous, and disposing every one to pensiveness and repose. Nor does the ode show minute or subtle observation, such as distinguishes much of the nature poetry of the present century. The objects and aspects described are obvious and common. The exquisite fineness in the poem is fineness of feeling and expression, not of perception. We should not expect Collins, the dreamer and visionary, to have a particularly keen eye for the facts of the external world. And in this poem, as elsewhere, he was more dreaming than seeing ; or, more accurately, he *was* seeing, but only because in this case seeing and dreaming were nearly one, nature at twilight creating a fairy world much like his own land of dreams. In other words, Collins did know and greatly love the common phenomena of evening, for the reason that they were peculiarly congenial to his mood and closely akin to that imaginary world in which his fancy loved to dwell.

As confirming this view, note how Collins mingles in the poem the facts of nature with his own and others' fancies. The sun and the hours are persons, as in old mythology. Elves, and nymphs who shed the dew, and Pensive Pleasures sweet, prepare Evening's shadowy car. Even the conventional personifications with which the poem ends show only the same tendency carried farther ; fancy banishes fact altogether, and nothing is left but the group of wooden abstractions, stiffly sitting in the "sylvan shed." This sorry ending is simply a striking proof of the fact that Collins, in this poem, had no thought of making an objective study of nature, still less of founding a new school of nature poetry. He was not trying, in Wordsworth's phrase, to keep his eye

" steadily on the object." Rather he was attracted instinctively to the dreamy aspects of twilight, partly for their own sake, and partly because they made so poetic a habitation for the creatures of his imagination.; and so he wrote a poem in which the two series of facts, the real and the imaginary, freely intermingled, although they never became identified. In all this there was nothing new in kind. He was simply at his old trick of dreaming again, only in this instance it was evening, instead of the wars on the continent or the literature of terror, that supplied the inspiration and part of the material.

If this be true, we should expect to find it true at the core of the poem, in the conception of evening itself. And it is true there. Throughout the ode, *Evening* and *evening* are distinct, and Collins's attention is divided between the two. Whole stanzas are given up to natural description, without the slightest immediate reference to Evening the person. At other times Evening is directly addressed, but rather frigidly and in terms which only in the most general way suggest a connection with the objective facts; as " chaste Eve," " nymph reserved," " maid composed," " calm votaress," and " meekest Eve." In a few places the relation is more intimate, and the personification more imaginative, notably in

and in
> Prepare thy shadowy car,

> marks o'er all
> Thy dewy fingers draw
> The gradual dusky veil.

But the person and the phenomena are never completely fused, as might have happened had Collins been wholly absorbed in picturing the scenes of the real world at evening time. Keats, in his ode to Autumn, was thus absorbed in catching up into words the subtle spirit of the " season of mists and mellow fruitfulness," and he has identified Autumn the person with autumn the season. Autumn in his poem is no sturdy matron with sickle and sheaf. She is the haunting spirit of the " granary floor," the " half-reaped furrow," and the oozing cider-press. She has no fixed body, but many flitting incarnations, in which " whoever seeks abroad " may catch glimpses of her very essence. In the *Ode to Evening* there is no such inner unity. Collins was at once describing the appearances of nature at his favorite hour of twilight and writing an ode to the personified spirit of the hour. The spirit was as real to him as the hour, and probably he would not have cared to identify the two. The thought of a semi-supernatural being, beautiful, ethereal, the goddess-queen of twilight, dim-flitting in delicate majesty through her shadowy realm, was of just the sort to captivate the imagination of Collins. He must have loved with delicate intensity the natural phenomena of evening; but they doubtless took on additional charm when he thought of them as the drapery and chariot and dim fairyland of the mystic Spirit of Twilight. And so it probably never occurred to him that this poem on evening was materially different in motive or method from his other odes. Just as in the *Ode to Fear* he pictured an imaginary world of terror as the dwelling-place for his " mad nymph," so in the *Ode to Evening* he merely took, ready made to his hand by nature, the world of twilight as the realm of his " maid composed."

The poem has, therefore, a perfectly definite and normal relation to the qualities of Collins's mind and to his usual poetic method. Wherein, then, does its uniqueness consist? Precisely in this happy combination of delicate fancy with delicate fact, and in the singular felicity with which the elusive, dissolving appearances of twilight are described in words as magical as themselves. In short, the right subject had found the right poet.

In its relation to Romanticism the *Ode to Evening* is as

remarkable in one way as the *Ode to Fear* is in another.
The descriptive parts of the poem are entirely romantic in
their intense though delicate passion for some of the loveliest aspects of nature, and in the fidelity, born of love, with
which those aspects are delineated. It is interesting to
compare the ode with the description of evening in the
third eclogue:

> While ev'ning dews enrich the glitt'ring glade,
> And the tall forests cast a longer shade.[1]

The lines are as conventional as they well could be; they
show memory of other poets' phrases, not observation of the
real world. Contrast with them these lines from the ode:

> But when chill blust'ring winds, or driving rain,
> Forbid my willing feet, be mine the hut
>   That from the mountain's side
>   Views wilds, and swelling floods,
>
> And hamlets brown, and dim-discover'd spires,
> And hears their simple bell, and marks o'er all
>   Thy dewy fingers draw
>   The gradual dusky veil.

At the time when the *Persian Eclogues* were written, Collins
must already have learned to know and love the sights and
sounds of evening; but he had not yet felt that it was worth
while, in poetry, to try to paint the appearances of nature
as faithfully as possible, and that in fact anything else in
descriptions of nature was hardly worth doing at all. When,
in the *Ode to Evening*, he reached that point, not by theory
but by instinct and by happy accident in choice of subject,

---

[1] The next two lines, with their pleasant touches of local color, were
added in the second edition, which appeared fifteen years after the first;
they afford, therefore, additional proof of the change in Collins's
manner of describing nature:

> What time 't is sweet o'er fields of rice to stray,
> Or scent the breathing maize at setting day.

he had taken a step which English poetry in general was to take some years later.

The Classicism in the poetry of Collins is, at first glance, even more apparent than the Romanticism. It is present in all the poems, from earliest to latest, but may be most conveniently studied in the *Odes* of 1747, where it reached its highest development.

Collins's love for genuine classic art receives direct expression in the *Ode to Simplicity*, which draws its inspiration from Greek literature and not from the frigid Classicism of the age of Queen Anne. The same backward look appears in the many other allusions to Greek literature, art, and history. Collins's admiration for Milton, which is shown by frequent Miltonic echoes in style even more than by direct praise, resulted naturally from the combination of the classic and the romantic in his own ideal ; for Milton came nearer to realizing such an ideal than any other English poet. It was natural that a poet of Collins's tastes and literary environment, groping about for a richer poetic method, yet appreciating all that was good in the classical ideals of the day and drawn powerfully towards the truer Classicism of ancient art, should turn to the author of *Lycidas* and *Paradise Lost* as his exemplar and guide. The last of the great Elizabethans satisfied at once his love of classic finish and his hunger for richness, imagination, and lofty passion.

In practice Collins's classic instincts appear partly in a certain restraint in the handling of romantic subject-matter, which he never allows to run away with him into extravagance or disproportion. This restraint was the easier, however, because his romantic material was comparatively meagre and tame. But his Classicism appears chiefly in constant qualities of verse, style, and general manner. The *Odes* are characterized by a repose, an economy of expression, and a purity of outline which suggest Greek sculpture, the pictures of Raphael, or the tapestries of Mantegna. Even where the style is involved, as in some of the longer odes, the total effect is simple — the threads may be curiously interwoven, but the resulting figure is clear and restful ; while many of the shorter odes have the snow-pure limbs of a statue fresh from the sculptor's chisel. The versification of the *Odes* is finished and careful. Collins exercised considerable freedom in the choice of stanza-forms ; but, having chosen them, he adhered to them. Within the individual line he admitted but few variations, and those usually consisted merely of a shifting of accent in the first foot. A freedom in the placing of cæsuras, never degenerating into license or caprice, contributes its part to the total effect of Collins's verse at its best, an effect which may be briefly described as a combination of polish with variety, richness, and ease.

The *Ode on the Death of Mr. Thomson*, published two years and a half later than the *Odes* of 1747, bears evidence that Collins had not gone backward in his poetic development. In their sincerity and naturalness the verses are separated by a great gulf from the conventional elegy of the day. In feeling and manner they are purely lyric ; something of the motion of the "lorn stream" itself flows in gentle sadness through the lines. The world of legend and fancy in which Collins loved to wander gleams out here and there — in the name of "druid" given to Thomson, in the allusion to the harp of Æolus, in the foot-note referring to Thomson's most romantic poem ; while the lines

> And see, the fairy valleys fade ;
> Dun night has veil'd the solemn view,

recall the *Ode to Evening* in their combination of fancy with one of the most romantic phases of nature.

But it is not till we turn to the *Ode on the Popular Superstitions of the Highlands of Scotland* that we realize how far

Collins had advanced in the theory and practice of Romanticism during the three years that followed the publication of the earlier *Odes.*

Scattered through the poem are several expressions showing the belief now held by Collins about the new class of subjects for poetry. Something of the old apologetic tone lingers still. He thinks it necessary to exhort Home, " though learned," not to forget the " homelier thoughts " of the " untutored swain." He props up the cause of Romanticism by citing the examples of Tasso, Fairfax, Spenser, and Shakspere. And in one instance he adopts language still more apologetic :

> Nor need'st thou blush, that such false themes engage
> Thy gentle mind, of fairer stores possest.

But it would appear that in these passages Collins was merely seeking to conciliate his opponents in poetic theory ; for in other lines he shows enthusiastic faith in the poetic value of the new subject-matter, and makes a just distinction between the imaginative and the false :

> Let thy sweet Muse the rural faith sustain:
> These are the themes of simple, sure effect,
> That add new conquests to her boundless reign,
> And fill, with double force, her heart-commanding strain.
>
> In scenes like these, which, daring to depart
> From sober truth, are still to nature true.

It is evident that Collins had even come to realize that it was just this kind of food which his own genius had needed for its full development ; and there is a touch of pathos in his gentle envy of Home for having the good fortune to be born in " Fancy's land," far from the barren conventionalism of literary England :

> Fresh to that soil thou turn'st, whose ev'ry vale
> Shall prompt the poet, and his song demand :
> To thee thy copious subjects ne'er shall fail ;
> Thou need'st but take the pencil to thy hand,
> And paint what all believe who own thy genial land.

Still more remarkable is the absence of the didactic point of view. In the *Eclogues*, and even in the *Odes* of 1747, didacticism still clung to the skirts of the poet's magic mantle. In this ode the superstitions of the Highlands are not recommended because they could be used to point a moral, but wholly for their intrinsic poetical qualities. They "call forth fresh delight to Fancy's view." These themes of "simple, sure effect" are valued because they can the "answering bosom pierce." Fairfax's poetry is praised, not because it taught truth and morality, but because "at each sound imagination glows" and the verse "fills the impassioned heart and wins the harmonious ear." Here is advance indeed since the days of the *Persian Eclogues*, when Hassan's camels were hitched to the dog-cart of a prudential morality.

Most significant of all is the imaginative abandon with which Collins throws himself into these superstitions of the North. This is particularly noticeable in the stanzas about the water-fiend and his hapless victim. Even the theory of Romanticism is for a time forgotten; and the ghost of the drowned man, with "blue-swollen face," and "shivering cold," stands before the mind's eye with all the vividness and realism of popular superstition.

This part of the ode, and the sketch of the simple inhabitants of St. Kilda, also anticipated in some degree that sympathetic and truthful portrayal of the lives of the poor which was to characterize so much of the poetry of Burns, Crabbe, and Wordsworth. The picture of island life is of course roseate compared with the stern realism of *The Parish Register* or the poetic homeliness of *Michael ;* but in com-

parison with the conventional descriptions of rural life in
the *Persian Eclogues* it shows a considerable advance in
naturalness and truth.

Collins's own style and method reveal the same progress in
Romanticism. The stanza is a rather shapeless and clumsy
enlargement of the Spenserian; and the style at times is
decidedly Spenser-like in diffuse picturesqueness or in delicate luxury of color :

> For, watchful, lurking 'mid th' unrustling reed,
> At those mirk hours the wily monster lies,
> And listens oft to hear the passing steed,
> And frequent round him rolls his sullen eyes,
> If chance his savage wrath may some weak wretch surprise.

> Yet frequent now, at midnight's solemn hour,
> The rifted mounds their yawning cells unfold,
> And forth the monarchs stalk with sov'reign pow'r,
> In pageant robes, and wreath'd with sheeny gold,
> And on their twilight tombs aërial council hold.

In not a few lines Collins has followed his own advice to
Home to suit his style to his romantic subject-matter and
" proceed in forceful sounds and colours bold." An instance
occurs in the third stanza :

> At ev'ry pause, before thy mind possest,
> Old Runic bards shall seem to rise around,
> With uncouth lyres, in many-colour'd vest,
> Their matted hair with boughs fantastic crown'd.

The style of the poem as a whole strikes one as having
more of romantic warmth and dash, and less of classical
finish, than any other of Collins's odes; but, as regards the
comparative lack of finish, it should be remembered that we
have only an imperfect first draught.

The limitations and the distinctive quality of the Romanticism in the poetry of Collins have already been implied ;
but they may now be briefly stated. Many of the romantic

aspects of nature, the picturesque in humble life, the picturesque in the feudal past, and the whole world of concrete
human passion and struggle either are entirely absent from
Collins's verse or receive only incidental and rudimentary
treatment. His Romanticism was that of an idealist with
strong classical tendencies, and anything which does not
blend readily with the classical and the ideal could not
enter his pages. It is a tempting problem what would have
been his poetical development had he lived, with faculties
unimpaired, for a generation longer. On the one hand, his
letter in 1750, in its reference to his new ode on the music
of the Grecian theatre, shows how highly he still valued
" correct " composition modelled upon the Greek classics.
On the other hand, so rapid had been his progress in
Romanticism during the brief interval between the *Odes* of
1747 and the *Ode on the Popular Superstitions of the Highlands* that it is probable that he would have moved with ever
increasing speed toward the bolder and wider Romanticism
reached even in his own century by Chatterton and Blake.

The influence of Collins upon the development of the
Romantic Movement in England was indefinite and slight.
This was chiefly due to the loss, for more than a generation,
of his most romantic poem. Had the *Ode on the Popular
Superstitions of the Highlands* been given to the world in 1749
instead of in 1788, it could not have failed to exert a powerful influence upon the growth of English Romanticism ; for,
as Professor Phelps has remarked, "it struck a new note in
English verse," and was "the first important poem " in that
branch of Romanticism which dealt with " native superstitions or Teutonic mythology." [1] As it was, we can do little
more than guess at the quiet effect which the published
poems of Collins may have wrought upon the poets of his own
and the succeeding generation. We may think that we detect

[1] *Beginnings of the English Romantic Movement*, p. 137.

the atmosphere of the *Ode to Evening* in the *Elegy Written in
a Country Churchyard;* the influence of the more elaborate
odes upon Gray's Pindarics ; an echo of the *Oriental
Eclogues* in Chatterton's *African Idylls;* possibly a trace of
The Passions in Beattie's *Ode to Hope,* and of the *Ode on the
Poetical Character* in the same poet's conception, in *The
Minstrel,* of the poetic temperament. But these and like
surmises are at best a scant and shadowy harvest. And
when the *Ode on the Popular Superstitions of the Highlands* finally came to light, it could no longer do the work of
a pioneer, but was, instead, a prophecy fulfilled ; while to a
later generation still, the name of Collins was a pitiful and
indignant memory, not an inspiration to new deeds in poesie.
Wordsworth, at the threshold of his poetic career, prayed

> that never child of song
> May know that poet's sorrows more.[1]

And Scott, looking back with the tenderness of a robust
nature for a delicate and unfortunate one, recognized the
kinship between himself and " Collins, ill-starred name,"
who loved

> to tread enchanted strand,
> And thread . . . the maze of Fairyland ;
> Of golden battlements to view the gleam,
> And slumber soft by some Elysian stream.[2]

But both Wordsworth and Scott found their inspiration
elsewhere than in the pages of Collins.

IV. THE POETRY OF COLLINS: AN APPRECIATION.

The poems other than the odes may be dismissed briefly.
Of the early minor poems only the *Song from Shakespear's
Cymbeline* has much interest for the reader of to-day ; that

---

[1] *Remembrance of Collins.*
[2] *The Bridal of Triermain,* Introduction.

will long be loved for its tenderness and graceful fancy. But the *Verses Written on a Paper* show a Miltonic richness of expression surprising in such a trifle ; and all the poems have a certain distinction, — a grace, finish, and freedom from the commonplace, — that was prophetic. They were prophetic in another way. Of these five little poems two are upon tears, one is a love plaint, and two are dirges. Evidently "the pert and nimble spirit of mirth" was not to preside over the poetry of Collins.

It is sufficiently high praise of the *Oriental Eclogues* to say that they can still be read. This not inconsiderable merit they owe to the narrative element, to the oriental setting, to the frequent prettiness of style and verse, and to the occasional fine strokes in description. The first eclogue is the least interesting. Its didacticism is but slightly relieved by the fiction of Selim and the maids of Bagdat; too evidently he exists only to preach and they exist only to listen. The second eclogue is the most graphic; but it is difficult to sympathize with the whining Hassan — did he expect to find the desert carpeted and the tigers caged ? The third eclogue is the prettiest of the series ; the *motif*, though slight, is sufficient and beautiful. As a pastoral the poem has an advantage which most romantic pastorals lack: the idealization of rural life is natural here, for we are looking through the eyes of characters who view that simple life from "midst the blaze of courts" and "thorns of state." In the last eclogue are the rudiments of a striking study in chiaroscuro ; but as a whole the picture is too general, and the modern reader is unable to believe in the woes of two such expert rhetoricians as the afflicted shepherds prove themselves to be.

The *Epistle Addressed to Sir Thomas Hanmer* can hardly be called dead, for it was stillborn. As poetry, save for a line or two, it is naught ; its learning is amateurish ; its literary criticism is conventional, and in one instance glaringly false. Collins had attempted the battle of Pope without Pope's weapons.

The odes are unequal in merit and interest ; but they have certain elements in common, which may be spoken of first.

There is a tendency nowadays, especially in comparisons of Collins with Gray, to overrate the purely lyric quality in the poetry of the former. Compared with contemporary poets, he had a conspicuous lyrical gift. But to ears accustomed to the wizard strains of Coleridge, the Ariel-like harpings and skylark flights of Shelley, and the passionate harmonies of Swinburne the music of Collins's lines seems comparatively commonplace and cold. His verse never soars, and it does sometimes stumble or creep. Its best qualities are finish, ease, and a certain quiet purity and richness. Collins plays a flute of clear and mellow tone.

Collins's style excels in picturesque and sculpturesque effects. In the mind's eye he saw ideal scenes and forms with wonderful clearness, and with few strokes he could describe what he saw. One may or may not be interested in the picture or bas-relief, but one cannot fail to see it. The classic purity, conciseness, and repose of the style of the odes are doubly grateful nowadays, in contrast with the carelessness of the century's early romanticists and the painful " preciousness " of *fin-de-siècle* æsthetes. Collins's style is at once natural and artful ; and occasionally it combines ease with compact richness in passages that remind one of the early style of Milton. In other places, especially in the *Ode on the Popular Superstitions of the Highlands,* his growing Romanticism shows itself in a restrained warmth of color somewhat after Spenser's best manner. But it must be confessed that not infrequently the style of the odes is commonplace and flat.

The imagination of Collins was limited in range. His

vision was confined almost wholly to ideal abstractions, to the supernatural, to a few phases of nature allied to the ideal or the supernatural, and to periods in the world's history and literature embodying his ideals of art and freedom. And in effect his range was even narrower than would appear from this enumeration ; for the most prominent objects before his mind's eye were the ideal abstractions, round which gathered his thoughts upon art, freedom, nature, and the supernatural. This lack of grasp upon concrete reality, upon human and dramatic interest, is the chief reason why the poetry of Collins never has been popular and never can be. "The defect of his poetry in general," says Craik, "is that there is too little of earth in it : in the purity and depth of its beauty it resembles the bright blue sky."[1] But his personified abstractions are usually saved from emptiness and frigidity by his habit of associating with them concrete facts illustrative of the quality in hand. Thus we know Liberty by Greece, Switzerland, and Britain; Fear, by storms, tragedy, and ghosts.

Collins's thought had about the same limitations as his imagination, for he seems to have thought chiefly in images. His purely intellectual power was not remarkable. He had apparently meditated more upon questions of literary theory than upon any other topic ; and even here he shows, in general, fine feeling rather than originality or depth of thought. It should, however, be remembered that at the time when he wrote most of his odes Collins was still a very young man. His enthusiasm for liberty seems to have proceeded rather from instinct than from reflection ; it was a part of his freedom-loving temperament, which showed itself also in his life and in his departure from literary conventions. In brief, one sees many pictures in the pages of Collins, but does not receive much truth.

[1] *History of English Literature*, London, 1864, vol. II, p. 284.

The passion in the odes is neither powerful nor of wide range, but it is always fine and sometimes exquisite. Collins was not a robust nature. He was mistaken if he really supposed himself capable of writing tragedy; that calls for sterner stuff than the delicate, sensitive horror of the terrible which palpitates through the *Ode to Fear*. But in pathos, and the tender emotions generally, the odes are rich. "Collins had skill to complain," wrote his first editor, who should be thankful to have said one good thing amid many foolish. This note of tenderness, of delicate pity blended with fancy, which vibrates again and again in Collins's verse and reveals a nature of remarkable purity and sensitiveness, is what chiefly endears him to the reader. Here at least he is human, although his tenderness is usually too ideal in form, too aloof from the beaten paths of life, to reach the popular heart like the tenderness of Burns or Longfellow.

The gentleness and repose of the poet's nature appear conspicuously in his steady love for the country life. Beginning with the *Eclogues*, the song about Damon, and the dirge for Fidele, he ended with the quiet woodland and river scenery of the stanzas on Thomson and with the sketch of Kilda's simple folk in the Highlands ode; while in the intermediate *Odes* of 1747, as M. Montégut has happily remarked, we see "une miniature d'Arcadie, d'où surgissent en abondance des images de paix, de repos, et de silence."[1] Collins's dislike of war and his love of peace breathe the same spirit. He even associates his beloved pastoral atmosphere with martial subjects, and, to quote again from the critic just named, is probably "le seul poète qui ait chantè l'héroisme et la vertu militaire sur le chalumeau, la *tenuis avena* de Tityre."[2]

---

[1] *Heures de Lecture d'un Critique*, Paris, 1891, p. 208.
[2] *Ibid.*

Three of the odes, *The Passions*, the *Ode to Evening*, and *How Sleep the Brave*, have attained to something of popularity and call for brief special comment.

The Passions, the most popular, is the least poetical of the three. In addition to the didacticism and the lack of unity commented upon elsewhere,[1] the poem is injured by a certain hollowness and declamatory tone. The imagination merely glances over the surface of the subject. In places it is difficult to escape the impression that we are witnessing a "performance," in which the Passions go through their appointed parts. Hope smiles and waves her golden hair, Melancholy plays upon the horn with pensive prettiness, Revenge beats the drum and strains his eyeballs. We look on unmoved. There is more of imaginative abandon in the lively lines about Cheerfulness and Joy. But in the tone of the poem as a whole may be found an explanation of the melancholy fact that as early as 1782 the ode had already become the victim of "frequent public recitals."[2] The merits of *The Passions* are considerable. The perfect clearness of the style, the easy if rather metallic and too obvious music of the verse, the purity and finish of the pictures, have doubtless combined with the declamatory manner to render the ode popular. Yet the fact remains that in delicacy of feeling and penetrative imagination it is inferior to several of the less popular poems.

The *Ode to Evening* is the most modern of Collins's poems, resembling, as has already been pointed out, the work of the impressionist school. But it was a favorite with lovers of poetry long before that school arose, and it will continue to be a favorite long after modern literary fashions shall have passed away. Although less popular than *The Deserted Village* and Gray's *Elegy*, the *Ode to Evening* is yet like them in embodying in exquisite form sights, sounds, and feelings

---

[1] See *Appendix, A*.   [2] See p. xxxvi.

of such permanent beauty that age cannot wither them nor custom stale. In all the finer qualities of poetry, — in unobtrusive melody, in nameless felicity of phrase, in fancy and imagination, in suggestive description, in feeling for the delicately beautiful in nature, — it is far superior, not only to the more strepitant ode on the Passions, but to nearly all of Collins's verse. Its sustained poetic tone is the more remarkable because of the introduction of homely details about the bat and beetle, which are taken up into the imaginative atmosphere of the poem and help to give it realism and distinction without loss of beauty or dignity. The ode will be read and loved so long as the sights and sounds of evening itself are loved by readers of English poetry.

In one respect, however, the *Ode to Evening* is sadly imperfect. The last three stanzas fall so far below the rest that the reader must either make for himself an ending, which is not a conclusion, at the fortieth line, or rise from the poem with an unpleasant sense of beauty marred by wooden conventionalism. There remains for mention, however, one poem not only exquisite in parts but perfect as a whole, a diamond of small size but of the finest quality and cutting. Pathos and fancy were perhaps never so successfully blended as in the lines *How Sleep the Brave*, which are themselves like a "knell" rung by "fairy hands." The mingled delicacy and majesty of the mourning figures, the ideality and truth in the three-word characterization of Spring, the sustained tone of repose, the combination of grace with economy and richness of expression, all these unite to form a whole of gentle but enduring charm. The little poem is perfect of its kind, and the kind is exquisite. A violet is not superior in daintiness, delicate precision of outline, and cool fragrance.

The poetry of Collins does not strive nor lift up its voice

in the streets.   But if it startles not, neither does it weary. Its Milton-like harmony of classic restraint with romantic richness secures it alike from extravagance and from frigid- ity.   Its purity of beauty is a lasting delight.   Already it has survived a century and a half, partly by reason of its significance in the history of English poetry, but chiefly because of intrinsic merit ; and there needs no special illu- mination to predict for the best of it a secure though quiet immortality.

APPENDIX.

———oo⁘oo———

A.

THE STRUCTURE OF THE ODES.

In Collins's day both the simple Horatian ode and the elaborate Pindaric had long been domesticated in English literature. Jonson (1573–1637) wrote odes in both forms. The structure of his ode to the memory of Sir Lucius Cary and Sir Henry Morison is modelled exactly upon the odes of Pindar, although he translated "strophe," "antistrophe," and "epode" into "turn," "counter-turn," and "stand."

Horatian odes were plentiful enough throughout the seventeenth century, but the Pindaric ode seems to have been wholly neglected until the time of Cowley (1618–1667). Cowley had a zeal for Pindarics, but not according to knowledge. Although he read Pindar in the original, he mistook the complexity of the metre for irregularity and lawlessness, saying in the preface to his *Pindaric Odes*, "though the grammarians and critics have laboured to reduce his [Pindar's] verses into regular feet and measures, . . . yet in effect they are little better than prose to our ears." Cowley-Pindarics were soon the rage. They became and long remained the favorite metre of poet-laureates in their official performances ; and in truth no form could be better adapted for making a pompous something out of nothing. The climax of combined tumidity and dullness was reached, perhaps, in the *Ode to the Creator of the World*, by John Hughes (1677–1720), who also paraphrased some of Horace's neat odes into great heaps of swelling emptiness.

To Congreve (1670–1729), as Johnson said, " we are indebted . . for the cure of our Pindaric madness." Congreve had himself been among the sinners, but in 1706 he came to a knowledge of the truth and brought forth fruits meet for repentance. In that year he published an ode entirely correct in form, and prefixed a *Discourse on the Pindaric Ode*, in which he said : " The following ode is an attempt towards restoring the regularity of the ancient lyric poetry, which seems to be altogether forgotten, or unknown, by our English writers. . . . The character of these late Pindarics is a bundle of rambling incoherent thoughts, expressed in a like parcel of irregular stanzas. . . . On the contrary, there is nothing more regular than the odes of Pindar."[1] From Congreve to Collins correct Pindaric odes were common, although the irregular Pindaric also continued to be written and published.

In a general way, therefore, it may be said that Collins was doing nothing new in writing odes. For both the simple and the elaborate form he had numerous models in English verse, besides the Latin and Greek originals. Even the unrhymed *Ode to Evening* repeated the stanza of Milton's translation of the *Fifth Ode* of Horace, in addition to being an imitation of a favorite metre of the Latin poet. The only thing worthy of note, so far as yet appears, is that amid the varying practice of the age Collins's classic taste led him to compose all his odes, with two exceptions, either in simple measures or in the exacting Pindaric form. One of the two exceptions is the *Ode on the Popular Superstitions of the Highlands ;* for a reference to the effect of Collins's growing Romanticism upon the stanza of this poem, see the *Introduction*, p. lv. The other exception is *The Passions*, the metre of which, although irregular, is far from lawless, as will be shown

---

[1] The following passage from the same preface affords an amusing illustration of the mental temper which was still possible in literary criticism to a distinguished man of letters: " What the origin was of these different motions and stations in singing their odes is not our present business to inquire. Some have thought that by the contrariety of the strophe and antistrophe they intended to represent the contra rotation of the *primum mobile* in respect of the *secunda mobilia ;* and that by their standing still at the epode they meant to signify the stability of the earth. Others ascribe the institution to Theseus, who thereby expressed the windings and turnings of the labyrinth, in cele brating his return from thence." — Chalmers's *English Poets*, London 1810, vol. X, pp. 300, 301.

later ; and even upon a superficial view the ode is far removed from the shapeless monsters that had been and were still masquerading as Pindarics.

As to subjects for odes, and manner of treatment, the greatest latitude prevailed in Collins's day.   Almost anything might be taken as the subject for an ode of the simple sort.   Collins's friend Joseph Warton wrote an *Ode to a Gentleman on his Travels* and an *Ode on Shooting.*   The odist usually contrived to address somebody or something, but in a meditative ode even this distinction might disappear.   The elaborate ode was more restricted in subject and manner.   Elevation was considered essential, and the effort to secure it often resulted in extravagance and bombast. Collins in both classes of his odes again showed his classical instinct by avoiding meanness or triviality, on the one hand, and absurdity on the other.   He is not always uniform.   *The Manners* has least elevation of subject and style; *The Passions* comes nearest to empty declamation ; the *Ode on the Poetical Character* approaches the borders of the unintelligible and merely fantastic. But on the whole it is within the truth to say that Collins's simple odes are never undignified, and his elaborate odes never turgid or absurd.

The simple odes, with one exception, do not here call for special study, as they exhibit nothing remarkable in structure or verse. The exception is the *Ode to Evening*, one of the few successful unrhymed lyrics in the English language.   Its musical charm is too subtle to yield up its innermost secret to cold analysis, but on attentive study some of the causes for its metrical success come to light.

The fundamental cause is the high poetic quality of the thought and feeling, which does not so much divert attention from the mere rhythm and sound as reduce the demands upon them, just as in the contrary case, in poems where the mind and eye are not gratified, the ear is the more importunate.   This may be tested in the last stanza, whose comparative poverty in metrical effect is due chiefly to poverty of thought.

Again, blank verse is peculiarly adapted to this poem, for the reason that the absence of rhyme-emphasis at the ends of the lines favors the fusing of line into line, an effect which subtly harmonizes with the attempt to describe the dissolving appearances of twilight. This effect is most definite in stanza 10, but it is present throughout the poem as a part of the atmosphere. The shortening of the last two lines in each stanza, by producing a "dying fall," contributes to a somewhat similar effect, as do also the occasional run-on lines and the several instances where stanza melts into stanza with only a comma between. As Hazlitt has said, "the sounds steal slowly over the ear, like the gradual coming on of evening itself."

Aside from imitative effects, the ode is richer than at first appears in elements of melody, rhythm, and stanzaic structure which go some way toward satisfying the sense for form without the aid of rhyme. It should first be noted, however, that in two stanzas rhyme itself is present. In stanza 5 the first line rhymes with the third; in stanza 6 a rhyme occurs in the middle of lines 3 and 4. But stray rhymes in a blank-verse poem must be considered as defects, because they are casual departures from the type, and raise expectations which are not elsewhere satisfied. Legitimate elements of melody, however, are numerous throughout the ode in the form of open vowels and pleasant consonants, many of them, moreover, coming at the ends of lines, where they are most needed as a partial substitute for rhyme. The most liquid of English sounds, *l*, occurs 79 times in the 52 lines ; in stanza 8 there is an average of nearly three *l*'s to the line, and an average of two *l*'s to the line in stanzas 5 and 12. Great variety in the placing of caesuras combines with the run-on lines and run-on stanzas to produce unusual fluidity of motion. Certain elements of stanza-structure appear in many places, and help to preserve the poem from the formlessness which is the great danger in unrhymed measures. The shortening of the lines in the second half of each stanza is a constant and powerful factor in producing a sense of stanza-form. The recurrence of "now" in stanzas 2, 3, and 4, "when" and "then" in stanzas 6 and 8, and the rather rhetorical use of "while" and "so long" in stanzas 11, 12, and 13, although they are logical and not metrical in their primary effect, yet indirectly reinforce the metrical structure. Alliteration does still more in strengthening rhythmic and stanzaic effects. Through several stanzas runs a sustained alliteration ; and although some of these alliterative effects are individually slight, the resulting total is considerable. Stanza 1 is thus threaded into a certain unity by *s* ; stanza 2, by *w* and *b* ; stanza 3, by *w*, *b*, and *s* ; stanza 10, by *d*. The more marked alliterations are not very numerous ; but it is noticeable that they often occur at or near the end of the stanza, where they are of most service in preventing a sense of metrical flatness (see stanzas 2, 3, 4, 7, 10, 11, 12).

Of the elaborate odes the *Ode to Mercy* is the shortest and the simplest in structure, resembling several of Pindar's odes in having no epode. The metrical scheme and the relation of the thought to it may be seen in the following outline :[1]

Ode to Mercy.

1. *Strophe:* Mercy's general characteristics.

2. *Antistrophe:* Mercy's special service to Britain.

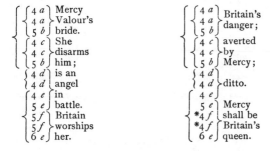

The *Ode to Fear* is, next to the Passions, the least regular of the odes. The epode should have been called a mesode, as it

---

[1] Figures indicate the number of feet in the line ; letters, the rhymes ; stars, feminine endings ; braces on the left of the columns of figures, metrical groups as determined by rhymes or line-lengths ; braces on the right of the columns of letters, divisions in the thought.

comes between strophe and antistrophe instead of after the latter. In the extant odes of Pindar there are no mesodes, but they sometimes occur in the choral odes of the Greek dramas.

ODE TO FEAR.

1. *Strophe :* Imaginative, descriptive characterization of Fear.

3. *Antistrophe :* Fear in nature, human life, folk-lore, and modern poetry.

4 a	} Fear	
4 a	imagi-	
4 b	native.	
4 b		
3 c	Fear	
3 c	comes,	
5 d	terrified,	
5 d	terrifying.	
5 c	Fear's train :	
4 e		
4 e		
4 f	Danger,	
4 f		
4 g		
4 g		
4 h	phantoms,	
4 h		
4 i	fiends,	
4 i		
4 j	vengeance,	
4 j		
4 k	Fate's	
4 k	hounds ;	
4 l	all	
4 l	terrible.	

4 a	} Fear	
4 a	weary.	
4 b	Fearful	
4 b	things	
3 c	in life	
3 c	and	
5 d	nature.	
5 d		
[ ]		
4 e	Fear	
4 e	in	
4 f	modern	
4 f	poetry	
4 g	and in	
4 g	folk-	
4 h	lore.	
4 h		
4 i		
4 i		
4 j		
4 j	Invoca-	
4 k	tion to	
4 k	Shakspere,	
4 l	Fear's	
4 l	greatest	
4m	prophet.	
4m		

2. *Epode :* Fear in Greek tragedy.

Five pentameter quatrains : Greek tragedy early and effective ; Æschylus ; Sophocles ; Fear the chief inspiration of Greek tragedy.

The *Ode on the Poetical Character* was printed in the original edition without divisional headings, although the epode and the antistrophe were indicated by the figures 2 and 3. Yet the ode is the most regular of the series.

ODE ON THE POETICAL CHARACTER.

1. *Strophe:* The magic girdle of poetry is for few.

3. *Antistrophe:* High poetry, like Milton's, is hard to attain unto.

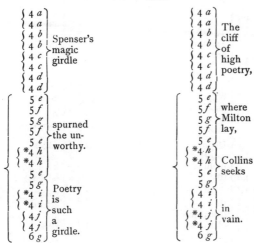

2. *Epode:* The weaving of the magic girdle of poetry.

Sixteen tetrameter couplets : Poetry and creation coeval; poetry is pure, wonderful, true, human and heavenly; who is sufficient for it?

The *Ode to Liberty* is the longest of the *Odes* of 1747, and with the exception of *The Passions* is the most varied in metre. It will be noticed that in strophe and antistrophe the second six lines repeat the rhyme-order of the first six, the line-lengths being also the same except in the case of the last lines. The concluding nine lines in strophe and antistrophe are identical with the Spenserian stanza in rhyme-order and in the length of the last line, although not in the other line-lengths. In the antistrophe, rhyme *j* is the same as rhyme *g*, probably by accident.

Ode to Liberty.

1. *Strophe:* Liberty in the ancient world.

3. *Antistrophe:* Britain torn from the mainland to be the last home of Liberty.

4 *a*	
4 *a*	The
*4 *b*	Spartan
5 *c*	heroes.
*5 *b*	
5 *c*	
4 *d*	The
4 *d*	Athe-
*5 *e*	nian
5 *f*	tyran-
*5 *e*	nicides.
6 *f*	
4 *g*	Depre-
4 *h*	catory
4 *g*	prelude
4 *h*	to
4 *i*	
4 *j*	the
5 *i*	overthrow
4 *j*	of Rome
4 *j*	by the
5 *k*	barba-
5 *j*	rians.
4 *k*	
6 *k*	

4 *a*	Prelude.
4 *a*	
*4 *b*	Britain
5 *c*	once a
*5 *b*	part
5 *c*	of the
4 *d*	main-
4 *d*	land.
*5 *e*	
5 *f*	A
*5 *e*	storm
6 *f*	arose,
4 *g*	which
4 *h*	made
4 *g*	it an
4 *h*	island,
4 *i*	with
4 *j*	attend-
5 *i*	ant
4 *j*	isles,
4 *j*	
5 *k*	to be
5 *j*	Liberty's
4 *k*	last
6 *k*	home.

2. *Epode:* Liberty in the modern world.

Nineteen tetrameter couplets; couplet 11 has feminine endings: Liberty has found a home in Italy, Switzerland, Holland, Britain.

4. *Second Epode.* — First Part: British liberty nearest the ideal; Second Part: Conclusion to the whole ode.

First Part. — Twenty tetrameter couplets; couplet 11 has feminine endings: The druids' temple of Liberty is gone, but the ideal model is still in heaven, combining ancient with modern elements, its walls graved with Britain's fame.

Second Part. — Eight tetrameter couplets: Britain, torn by wars, now craves peace with liberty.

From the above outlines it appears :

1.   That the metrical structure of the odes is in a general way regular, consisting of distinct parts having a definite relation to each other.

2.   That the metrical correspondence between similar parts is sometimes curiously exact, and sometimes only approximate.

3.   That the epode is always in uniform metre, while the strophe and the antistrophe are in more or less varied metre.

4.   That with one exception the epode always comes between strophe and antistrophe ; and that the exception arises merely from the presence of two epodes, one of which is in the usual intermediate position, while the other naturally follows the antistrophe.

5.   That large and distinct divisions in the thought always correspond to the large divisions in the metrical structure.

6.   That the smaller thought-divisions sometimes do and sometimes do not correspond with the smaller metrical divisions.

The significance of these facts will be pointed out later.

The structure of *The Passions* shows the influence of the Cowley-Pindaric ode, but it shows also how Collins's native sense for proportion and form restrained him from going to extremes even while he was experimenting, for once, with irregular measures.

The introduction and the conclusion, comprising 40 lines out of 118, are written in plain tetrameter couplets, and alone would suffice to give some degree of sanity and moderation to the metrical effect of the poem as a whole. The fifth and sixth lines of both introduction and conclusion have feminine endings, but this correspondence may have been accidental. Following the introduction come three quietly moving tetrameter quatrains. The broken measures then begin. But the first three lines are tetrameter still, although the feet in the second and third lines change to trochaic. Longer lines then creep in, and the description of Hope ends with two hexameters. The rhyme-scheme of the lines on Hope is irregular also ; but it receives a loose kind of unity, certainly a sense of completeness, from the fact that the last line rhymes with the first. It is also connected, perhaps by accident, with the preceding quatrain, its first line rhyming with the quatrain's first and third lines. The passage on Revenge is linked with that on Hope by its second rhyme. The rhyme-scheme follows no perceptible law, although it gains a little unity by the return of its fourth rhyme in the last line. Cunningly hidden in the middle of the passage is an unrhymed line (l. 45). The variety in line-lengths here is greater than elsewhere in the poem, the lines ranging from trimeters to hexameters. The appropriateness of the broken metre, especially the impatient short lines, in a description so full of "furious heat" is obvious. The smooth-flowing quatrain on Jealousy, which follows, is an agreeable relief. With the description of Melancholy the longer and more complex verse-periods begin again. Of the 12 lines given to Melancholy 4 are couplets and the rest are quatrains ; there are 3 pentameters and 9 tetrameters. The descriptions of Cheerfulness and Joy, with their companions, are written in metre appropriately varied and lively, but not intricate or fantastic. Line 85 is unrhymed.

The subject-matter of the ode consists of two sections very unequal in length and very different in nature. Everything before the conclusion is descriptive, and has to do with the Passions and their relation to Music. The conclusion is didactic, and has to do with Music alone. The poem is, therefore, inferior to the other odes in unity. Either the conclusion seems a divergent after-thought ; or, if it be taken as the original motive of the poem, one's first impression about the descriptive parts must be re-adjusted — they seemed to exist for their own sake, but it turns out that they are arguments to prove the superiority of ancient music. The descriptive portion by itself has only a slight and super-ficial unity. With a few trifling exceptions there is no interac-tion between the Passions, who are merely brought together and rather mechanically wait their turns to play. The order in which they are mentioned seems to have been determined by contrast and likeness and by the desire to end with a climax of gaiety.

What is the conclusion of the whole matter?

It is a commonplace that the Pindaric ode in English is an artificial exotic, of slight native force, and unable to reproduce the effects of its Greek original. The reason is obvious. The

Greek odes were accompanied by music and dancing, the singers moving to one side during the strophe, retracing their steps during the antistrophe (which was for that reason metrically identical with the strophe), and standing still during the epode. The ear was thus helped by the eye, and the divisions of the ode were distinct and significant. But in an English Pindaric the elaborate correspondences and differences between strophe, antistrophe, and epode are lost upon most readers, and even the critical reader derives from them a pleasure intellectual rather than sensuous.

But while this is true of thoroughly academic Pindarics like those of Gray, in which the peculiar metrical effects are minute, it is not altogether true of the rougher Pindarics of Collins. Collins was less scholarly than Gray, but he was bolder and more original ; and consciously or unconsciously he so constructed his odes that their organic parts stand out clearly distinct and produce effects analogous to those produced by the Greek ode. In brief, his method was, first, to make large divisions of the thought correspond to the large divisions of the form ; and, second, to throw out into relief the complex strophe and antistrophe by contrasting them with a simple epode. The reader may not perceive the minute correspondences in form between strophe and antistrophe, but he can hardly fail to feel that the two answer to one another in a general way by being varied and complex ; while the epode at once emphasizes this effect by contrast and produces an impression of its own analogous to that of the Greek epode, namely, an impression of relief and repose. For this reason, apparently, Collins placed his epode between the other two parts instead of after them, a practice for which he seems to have had no English precedent. In the same way we may account for his carelessness about the minuter correspondences in metre and in the adjustment of the smaller thought-groups to metrical groups. Sometimes he seems to have amused himself by a curious regularity in minutiae, but the larger impressions were all that he considered essential. In *The Passions* similar effects of contrast and repose are secured by beginning and ending with simple metre and by placing quiet quatrains here and there among the passages of wilder flight.

B.

REFERENCES TO COLLINS'S POETRY IN THE EIGHTEENTH CENTURY.

" Have you seen the works of two young authors, a Mr. Warton and Mr. Collins, both writers of odes? It is odd enough, but each is the half of a considerable man, and one the counterpart of the other. The first has but little invention, very poetical choice of expression, and a good ear. The second, a fine fancy, modelled upon the antique, a bad ear, great variety of words and images, with no choice at all. They both deserve to last some years, but will not." — Gray's letter to Wharton, Dec. 27, 1746.

" We remember to have seen an edition of these beautiful eclogues about fourteen years ago ; and if our memory does not fail us, they were then intituled *Persian Eclogues.* . . . The thoughts are appropriated [*sic*], the images wild and local, the language correct, and the versification harmonious. . . . With what strength of colouring is the beginning of this piece [the second eclogue] wrought up ! . . . We are much mistaken, if, in this little performance, we do not discover the elegance and the picturesque genius of the too much neglected author of *Odes on several Subjects, descriptive and allegorical.*" — *The Monthly Review,* June, 1757.

" Of Mr. Collins's *Oriental Eclogues* we gave some account in the sixteenth volume of our *Review,* page 486, and there we observed that his *Odes descriptive and allegorical* had been too much neglected. It shall not, however, be our fault if they are neglected any longer. If a luxuriance of imagination, a wild sub-limity of fancy, and a felicity of expression so extraordinary that it might be supposed to be suggested by some superior power, rather than to be the effect of human judgement or capacity, — if these are allowed to constitute the excellence of lyric poetry, the author of the *Odes descriptive and allegorical* will indisputably bear away the palm from all his competitors in that province of the Muse. . . . The *Ode on the Poetical Character* is so extremely wild and exorbitant that it seems to have been written wholly during the tyranny of imagination. Some, however, there are whose congenial spirits may keep pace with the poet in his most eccentric flights. . . . There is something perfectly classical in Mr. Collins's manner, both with respect to his imagery and his composition; and Horace's rule of *ut Pictura Poesis* was never better observed than in the above-quoted verses [*Ode to Mercy*, ll. 1–6]. . . . It is with peculiar pleasure that we do this justice to a poet who was too great to be popular, and whose genius was neglected because it was above the common taste." — *The Monthly Review*, January, 1764.

"The genius of Collins was capable of every degree of excellence in lyric poetry, and perfectly qualified for that high province of the Muse. Possessed of a native ear for all the varieties of harmony and modulation, susceptible of the finest feelings of tenderness and humanity, but above all, carried away by that high enthusiasm which gives to imagination its strongest colouring, he was, at once, capable of soothing the ear with the melody of his numbers, of influencing the passions by the force of his pathos, and of gratifying the fancy by the luxury of his description."— Langhorne, in his edition of Collins, London, 1765, p. 137.

"The grandeur of wildness, and the novelty of extravagance, were always desired by him, but not always attained. Yet, as diligence is never wholly lost, if his efforts sometimes caused harshness and obscurity, they likewise produced in happier moments sublimity and splendour. This idea which he had formed of excellence led him to oriental fictions and allegorical imagery, and perhaps, while he was intent upon description, he did not sufficiently cultivate sentiment. His poems are the productions of a mind not deficient in fire, nor unfurnished with knowledge either of books or life, but somewhat obstructed in its progress by deviation in quest of mistaken beauties. . . . His diction was often harsh, unskilfully labored, and injudiciously selected. He affected the obsolete when it was not worthy of revival; and he puts his words out of the common order, seeming to think, with some later candidates for fame, that not to write prose is certainly to write poetry. His lines commonly are of slow motion, clogged and impeded with clusters of consonants. As men are often esteemed who cannot be loved, so the poetry of Collins may sometimes extort praise when it gives little pleasure." — Johnson in his *Lives of the Poets*, London, 1820, pp. 268, 271. (The volume containing the life of Collins was published first in 1779.)

" A subscription is about to be set on foot, for the purpose of erecting a monument to that much-neglected but admirable bard, Collins, in the cathedral church of this his native city. His incomparable *Ode on the Passions* will furnish a design, which is to be executed in the best manner by that ingenious artist Flaxman. If any of your numerous correspondents can give information, through the medium of your useful Miscellany, whether any portrait or engraving of this venerable poet is extant, and how a sight of it may be obtained, the information will be thankfully received." — " W. G.," in *The Gentleman's Magazine*, December, 1789.

> YE ! WHO THE MERITS OF THE DEAD REVERE,
> WHO HOLD MISFORTVNE SACRED, GENIVS DEAR,
> REGARD THIS TOMB ! WHERE COLLINS, HAPLESS NAME !
> SOLICITS KINDNESS, WITH A DOVBLE CLAIM :
> THO' NATVRE GAVE HIM, AND THO' SCIENCE TAVGHT,
> THE FIRE OF FANCY, AND THE REACH OF THOVGHT,
> SEVERELY DOOM'D TO PENVRY'S EXTREME,
> HE PASS'D IN MADD'NING PAIN LIFE'S FEVERISH DREAM ;
> WHILE RAYS OF GENIVS ONLY SERV'D TO SHEW
> THE THICK'NING HORROR, AND EXALT HIS WOE.
> YE WALLS THAT ECHOED TO HIS FRANTIC MOAN,
> GVARD THE DVE RECORD OF THIS GRATEFVL STONE !
> STRANGERS TO HIM, ENAMOVR'D OF HIS LAYS,·
> THIS FOND MEMORIAL OF HIS TALENTS RAISE ;
> FOR THIS THE ASHES OF A BARD REQVIRE,
> WHO TOVCH'D THE TENDEREST NOTES OF PITY'S LYRE :
> WHO IOIN'D PVRE FAITH TO STRONG POETIC POWERS,
> WHO IN REVIVING REASON'S LVCID HOVRS,
> SOVGHT ON ONE BOOK HIS TROVBLED MIND TO REST,
> AND RIGHTLY DEEM'D THE BOOK OF GOD THE BEST.

— *Collins's Epitaph in Chichester Cathedral.*[1]

[1] Most printed transcripts of the epitaph contain several small errors. The above text is copied from the original in Chichester Cathedral. The bas-relief and epitaph together cover a large marble slab, which is affixed to a pier in the north aisle of the nave.

C.

BIBLIOGRAPHY.

Down to the end of the eighteenth century the list of editions of Collins has been made as complete as possible. Of editions belonging to the present century only the more valuable are named. With the exceptions indicated, all the works mentioned are in the British Museum. The other statements as to the location of editions are not meant to be taken as exhaustive.

Persian Eclogues. Written originally for the Entertainment of the Ladies of Taurus. And now first translated, &c. London : Printed for J. Roberts, in Warwick-Lane, 1742. (Price Sixpence.) 8vo.

> Not in the British Museum. One of the two copies in the Dyce Collection, in the South Kensington Museum, contains, on the fly-leaf facing the title-page, this entry in Dyce's hand : " This copy was given by Collins to Joseph Warton (see note by the latter on the back of the title page). The motto from Virgil on the title-page, the corrections, etc., are in the handwriting of Collins." The note on the back of the title-page is as follows : " Mr. Collins gave me this Copy with his own Hands when I & my Brother visited Him for the last time at Chichester." On the title-page, after " translated, &c.," is written in Collins's hand, " — Quos primus equis Oriens afflavit, anhelis." Below in the same hand, and cancelled with ink, are the words, " Equis Oriens afflavit anhelis." The quotation from Cicero (see p. 84) follows, but is crossed out with ink. The imprint is also crossed out. At the bottom of the title-page, in the same hand as that of the note on the back of the page, is this entry : " By Mr. Collins. (written at Winchester School) " For the written corrections of the text, see pp. 85, 90. This copy does not contain the *Preface ;* the other copy does.

Verses Humbly Address'd to Sir Thomas Hanmer. On his Edition of Shakespear's Works. By a Gentleman of Oxford. London : Printed for M. Cooper, in Paternoster Row, 1743. (Price Six Pence.) Folio.

An Epistle : addresst to Sir Thomas Hanmer, On his Edition of Shakespear's Works. The second edition. To which is added, A Song from the Cymbeline of the same Author. By Mr. William Collins, of Magdalene-College in Oxford. London : Printed for R. Dodsley, . . . and Mr. Cooper, . . . MDCCXLIV. (Price One Shilling.) Folio.

In the Dyce Collection in the South Kensington Museum. Not in the British Museum.

The Museum : or, the Literary and Historical Register. Volume the First. London : Printed for R. Dodsley, in Pall-Mall. MDCCXLVI.

No. VI, June 7, contains the *Ode to a Lady.* In the Library of Harvard University.

Odes on several Descriptive and Allegoric Subjects. By William Collins. [The motto from Pindar follows ; see p. 33.] London: Printed for A. Millar, in the Strand. MDCCXLVII. (Price One Shilling.) 8vo.

In the Library of Harvard University.

A Collection of Poems. By Several Hands. In Three Volumes. London : Printed for R. Dodsley, at Tully's Head in Pall-Mall. MDCCXLVIII.

The second edition contains the *Ode to a Lady,* the *Ode to Evening,* and *How Sleep the Brave.* The *Collection* was reprinted in 1763, 1765, 1767, 1783. Sometimes unauthorized changes were made in the text of the odes by Collins ; and some of the changes have been retained in later editions of the poet.

Ode Occasion'd by the Death of Mr. Thomson. By Mr. William Collins. *Haec tibi semper erunt, & cum solennia Vota reddemus Nymphis, & cum lustrabimus Agros. — Amavit nos quoque Daphnis.* Virg. Bucol. Eclog. v. London : Printed for R. Manby and H. S. Cox, on Ludgate-Hill. MDCCXLIX. [Price Six-pence.] [On the next leaf :] To George Lyttleton, Esq., this Ode is inscrib'd by the Author. Folio.

In the Dyce Collection in the South Kensington Museum. Not in the British Museum.

The Union : or, Select Scots and English Poems. . . . Edinburgh :
Printed for Archibald Munro & David Murray. MDCCLIII.

> Contains the *Ode to Evening* and the *Ode on the Death of Mr. Thomson*.

Oriental Eclogues. [For the rest of the title, etc., see p. 7.]
London : Printed for J. Payne, at Pope's Head, in Pater-
noster-Row. MDCCLVII. (Price One Shilling.) 4to.

> In the Library of Harvard University and the Boston Public
> Library.

The Poetical Calendar. Containing a Collection of scarce and
valuable Pieces of Poetry : With Variety of Originals and
Translations, by the Most Eminent Hands. . . . Written
and Selected by Francis Fawkes, M.A., and William Woty.
In twelve volumes. London : . . . 1763.

> In vol. XI are the *Oriental Eclogues*, the *Odes* of 1747, the
> *Epistle to Hanmer*, and the *Song from Shakespear's Cymbeline ;* in
> vol. XII, the *Ode on the Death of Mr. Thomson*, a sketch of
> Collins's life (with the lines *To Miss Aurelia C——R*), and John-
> son's description of his character.

The Poetical Works of Mr. William Collins. With Memoirs of
the Author ; and Observations on his Genius and Writings.
By J. Langhorne. . . . London : Printed for T. Becket and
P. A. Dehondt, at Tully's Head, near Surry Street, in the
Strand. MDCCLXV. 8vo.

> Contains all the poems now attributed to Collins, except the *Ode
> on the Popular Superstitions of the Highlands, Verses Written on a
> Paper, To Miss Aurelia C——R*, the *Sonnet*, and the *Song* about
> Damon. The text is eclectic. Some of its blunders or unauthor-
> ized changes have been reproduced again and again down to within
> recent years, as most subsequent editions were based upon this
> edition. Dyce says Langhorne's *Collins* was reprinted in 1771. In
> the Dyce Collection, in the South Kensington Museum, is an
> edition published in 1776. Still another reprint appeared in 1781.

The Poetical Works of Mr. William Collins. To which are added
Mr. Hammond's Elegies. Glasgow : Printed by Robert &
Andrew Foulis. MDCCLXXI. 18mo.

> Reprinted in 1777.

The Poetical Works of Mr. William Collins. To which are added, Mr. Hammond's Elegies. Edinburgh : Printed for J. Balfour and W. Creech. MDCCLXXIII. 8vo.

> This is vol. XLIII in the *British Poets* (same imprint).

A Collection of Poems, in four volumes. By Several Hands. London : Printed for G. Pearch, . . . MDCCLXXV. [Third edition.] 8vo.

> Vol. II contains the *Oriental Eclogues,* the odes on *Thomson, Pity, Simplicity, Peace, Mercy, Liberty, Fear,* and the *Poetical Character, The Manners, The Passions,* and *Verses Written on a Paper.*

The Works of the English Poets. With Prefaces, Biographical and Critical, by Samuel Johnson. Volume the Forty-Ninth. London : . . . MDCCLXXIX. 8vo.

> Collins's poems, with Langhorne's *Observations,* come last in the volume, preceded by Thomson's and Hammond's. Reprinted in 1790.

The Poetical Works of William Collins. With the Life of the Author. Edinburgh, 1781. 12mo.

> In vol. LXXXVIII of Bell's *Poets of Great Britain,* complete from Chaucer to Churchill; printed for John Bell, British Library, Strand, London, 1781. Reprinted in 1787.

The Poetical Works of William Collins. Glasgow : Printed by Andrew Foulis, Printer to the University. 1787. Folio.

> This edition contains a few plates, a life of Collins stolen from Langhorne's edition, and variant readings in the *Ode to a Lady* and the *Ode to Evening.*

Transactions of the Royal Society of Edinburgh. Vol. I. Edinburgh : . . . Sold in London by T. Cadell, in the Strand. MDCCLXXXVIII.

> Part II, Papers of the Literary Class, pp. 63–75, contains the *Ode on the Popular Superstitions of the Highlands of Scotland.* In the Library of Harvard University.

An Ode on the Popular Superstitions of the Highlands of Scotland ; considered as the Subject of Poetry. Inscribed to Mr.

Home, Author of Douglas. By Mr. William Collins, Author of the Ode on the Passions, &c. Never before printed. Dedicated to the Wartons. [The sentence, in Johnson's life of Collins, about the ode, follows.] London : Printed by J. Bell, Bookseller to His Royal Highness the Prince of Wales, at the British Library, Strand. 1788. 4to.

A second edition appeared in 1789.

The Poetical Works of William Collins. . . . To which is prefixed the Life of the Author. Edinburgh : 1794. 8vo.

In vol. IX of a *Complete Edition of the Poets of Great Britain*, published in London and Edinburgh, and edited by Robert Anderson.

Roach's Beauties of the Poets of Great Britain. . . . From the Works of the Most Admired Authors. In Six Volumes. London : 1794. 12mo.

Vol. IV contains *How Sleep the Brave*, the *Oriental Eclogues*, and the *Ode on the Poetical Character*.

Poems by William Collins, being Odes, descriptive and allegorical, etc. Colchester : . . . 1796. 12mo.

Annotated.

The Poetical Works of Mr. William Collins. With a Prefatory Essay by Mrs. Barbauld. London : . . . T. Cadell, jr. & W. Davies, . . . 1797. 8vo.

Reprinted in 1802.

The Poetical Works of William Collins, enriched with Elegant Engravings. . . . London : . . . E. Harding, . . . 1798. 8vo.

The Poetical Works of William Collins. . . . Embellished with Engravings from the Designs of Richard Westall, Esq., R. A. London : Printed . . . for John Sharpe. . . . 1804. 16mo.

A handsome edition. According to Dyce, the same edition, with a newly engraved title-page, and without the plates, was reprinted in 1811.

The Poetical Works of William Collins. Collated with the Best Editions : by Thomas Park, Esq., F. S. A. London : 1805. 16mo.

In vol. XXX of the *Works of the British Poets*, edited by Park. The most critical edition that had yet appeared, although some of the errors in Langhorne's text were retained.

The Poetical Works of William Collins ; with the Life of the Author by Dr. Johnson ; Observations on his Writings by Dr. Langhorne ; and Biographical and Critical Notes, by the Rev. Alexander Dyce, A.B. Oxon. London, William Pickering, Chancery Lane ; D. A. Talboys, Oxford. MDCCCXXVII.

Very valuable, although a collection of material rather than a finished edition. In the Boston Public Library.

The Poetical Works of William Collins. London : William Pickering. 1830. 8vo. [Aldine edition of the British Poets.]

Contains a biographical sketch based chiefly on Dyce's material, an *Essay on the Genius and Poems of Collins,* by Sir Egerton Brydges, Langhorne's *Observations,* and variant readings. In the Aldine editions of 1858, 1866, and 1894, Brydges's *Essay* and Langhorne's *Observations* were dropped, and a revised biographical sketch displaced the earlier one.

The Poems of William Collins, a New Edition, with a Critical Preface by Sir Egerton Brydges, Bart. Geneva : 1832. 16mo.

The preface is not the same as the essay in the Aldine edition of 1830.

The Poetical Works of William Collins. [The poems of Gray, Parnell, Matthew Green, and T. Warton in the same volume.] Edited by the Rev. Robert Aris Willmott. Illustrated. London : Routledge & Co. 1854. 8vo.

An eclectic and critical text, and some excellent notes.

Lectures on the English Poets, by William Hazlitt.

A few pages upon Collins in *Lecture VI.*

The English Poets, edited by T. H. Ward, vol. III.

>   The critical preface to the selections from Collins is by Swinburne.

Lowell's Works, vol. IV.

>   The essay on Pope, pp. 3, 4, contains a few sentences upon Collins.

The Athenaeum, Jan. 5, 1856, p. 10 *et seq.*

Émile Montégut.   Heures de Lecture d'un Critique.   Paris : . . . 1891.

>   Pp. 162–233 are devoted to Collins.

EARLY MINOR POEMS.

THE POEMS OF COLLINS.

TO MISS AURELIA C——R

ON HER WEEPING AT HER SISTER'S WEDDING.

Cease, fair Aurelia, cease to mourn;
    Lament not Hannah's happy state;
You may be happy in your turn,
    And seize the treasure you regret.

With Love united, Hymen stands,   5
    And softly whispers to your charms,
" Meet but your lover in my bands,
    You 'll find your sister in his arms."

SONNET.

When Phoebe form'd a wanton smile,
    My soul, it reach'd not here !
Strange that thy peace, thou trembler, flies
    Before a rising tear !

From midst the drops my love is born,   5
    That o'er those eyelids rove :
Thus issu'd from a teeming wave
    The fabled queen of love.

SONG.

THE SENTIMENTS BORROW'D FROM SHAKESPEAR.

Young Damon of the vale is dead ;
    Ye lowland hamlets, moan :

2. Ye lowly hamlets, moan :   — Many editions.

A dewy turf lies o'er his head,
  And at his feet a stone.

His shroud, which death's cold damps destroy,   5
  Of snow-white threads was made :
All mourn'd to see so sweet a boy
  In earth forever laid.

Pale pansies o'er his corpse were plac'd,
  Which, pluck'd before their time,   10
Bestrew'd the boy, like him to waste,
  And wither in their prime.

But will he ne'er return, whose tongue
  Could tune the rural lay ?
Ah, no ! his bell of peace is rung,   15
  His lips are cold as clay.

They bore him out at twilight hour,
  The youth who lov'd so well :
Ah me ! how many a true-love shower
  Of kind remembrance fell !   20

Each maid was woe, but Lucy chief ;
  Her grief o'er all was tried :
Within his grave she dropp'd in grief,
  And o'er her lov'd one died.

VERSES

WRITTEN ON A PAPER WHICH CONTAIN'D A PIECE OF
BRIDE-CAKE GIV'N TO THE AUTHOR BY A LADY.

YE curious hands that, hid from vulgar eyes,
  By search profane shall find this hallow'd cake,

18. The youth belov'd so well :
    — *The* [*London*] *Public Advertiser*, March 7, 1788.

With virtue's awe forbear the sacred prize,
  Nor dare a theft, for love and pity's sake !

This precious relick, form'd by magic pow'r, 5
  Beneath the shepherd's haunted pillow laid,
Was meant by Love to charm the silent hour,
  The secret present of a matchless maid.

The Cyprian queen, at Hymen's fond request,
  Each nice ingredient chose with happiest art ; 10
Fears, sighs, and wishes of th' enamour'd breast,
  And pains that please, are mixt in ev'ry part.

With rosy hand the spicy fruit she brought
  From Paphian hills and fair Cythera's isle :
And temper'd sweet with these the melting thought, 15
  The kiss ambrosial, and the yielding smile ;

Ambiguous looks, that scorn and yet relent ;
  Denials mild, and firm unalter'd truth ;
Reluctant pride, and amorous faint consent ;
  And meeting ardours, and exulting youth. 20

Sleep, wayward god, hath sworn, while these remain,
  With flatt'ring dreams to dry his nightly tear ;
And chearful Hope, so oft invok'd in vain,
  With fairy songs shall sooth his pensive ear.

If, bound by vows to Friendship's gentle side, 25
  And fond of soul, thou hop'st an equal grace,
If youth or maid thy joys and griefs divide,
  O much intreated, leave this fatal place !

Sweet Peace, who long hath shunn'd my plaintive day,
  Consents at length to bring me short delight ; 30
Thy careless steps may scare her doves away,
  And Grief with raven note usurp the night.

A SONG FROM SHAKESPEAR'S CYMBELYNE.

SUNG BY GUIDERUS AND ARVIRAGUS OVER FIDELE,
SUPPOS'D TO BE DEAD.

To fair Fidele's grassy tomb
   Soft maids and village hinds shall bring
Each op'ning sweet, of earliest bloom,
   And rifle all the breathing spring.

No wailing ghost shall dare appear,   5
   To vex with shrieks this quiet grove:
But shepherd lads assemble here,
   And melting virgins own their love.

No wither'd witch shall here be seen,
   No goblins lead their nightly crew: 10
The female fays shall haunt the green,
   And dress thy grave with pearly dew.

The redbreast oft at ev'ning hours
   Shall kindly lend his little aid,
With hoary moss, and gather'd flow'rs,   15
   To deck the ground where thou art laid.

When howling winds, and beating rain,
   In tempests shake the sylvan cell,
Or midst the chace on ev'ry plain,
   The tender thought on thee shall dwell.   20

Each lonely scene shall thee restore,
   For thee the tear be duly shed:
Belov'd, till life could charm no more;
   And mourn'd, till Pity's self be dead.

ORIENTAL ECLOGUES.

WRITTEN ORIGINALLY FOR THE ENTERTAINMENT OF THE
LADIES OF TAURIS.   AND NOW TRANSLATED.

— Ubi primus equis Oriens adflavit anhelis.

— Virg. *Georg*. Lib. I.

THE PREFACE.[1]

IT is with the writings of mankind, in some measure, as with their complexions or their dress ; each nation hath a peculiarity in all these, to distinguish it from the rest of the world.

The gravity of the Spaniard, and the levity of the Frenchman, are as evident in all their productions as in their persons themselves ; and the style of my countrymen is as naturally strong and nervous, as that of an Arabian or Persian is rich and figurative.

There is an elegancy and wildness of thought which recommends all their compositions ; and our geniuses are as much too cold for the entertainment of such sentiments, as our climate is for their fruits and spices. If any of these beauties are to be found in the following *Eclogues*, I hope my reader will consider them as an argument of their being original. I received them at the hands of a merchant, who had made it his business to enrich himself with the learning, as well as the silks and carpets of the Persians. The little information I could gather concerning their author, was, that his name was Abdallah, and that he was a native of Tauris.

It was in that city that he died of a distemper fatal in those parts, whilst he was engaged in celebrating the victories of his favourite monarch, the great Abbas.[2] As to the *Eclogues* themselves, they give a very just view of the miseries and inconveniences, as well as the felicities, that attend one of the finest countries in the East.

The time of writing them was probably in the beginning of Sha Sultan Hosseyn's reign, the successor of Sefi or Solyman the second.

[1] In the Dyce Collection, in the South Kensington Museum, are two copies of the 1742 edition of the *Eclogues*, one with the *Preface* and the other without it.

[2] In the Persian tongue, Abbas signifieth " the father of the people." — C.

Whatever defects, as, I doubt not, there will be many, fall under the reader's observation, I hope his candour will incline him to make the following reflection :

That the works of Orientals contain many peculiarities, and that, through defect of language, few European translators can do them justice.

ECLOGUE THE FIRST.

SELIM ; OR, THE SHEPHERD'S MORAL.

Scene, a valley near Bagdat. *Time*, the morning.

"Ye Persian maids, attend your poet's lays,
And hear how shepherds pass their golden days.
Not all are blest, whom Fortune's hand sustains
With wealth in courts, nor all that haunt the plains :
Well may your hearts believe the truths I tell ;   5
'T is virtue makes the bliss, where'er we dwell."

Thus Selim sung, by sacred Truth inspir'd ;
Nor praise, but such as Truth bestow'd, desir'd :
Wise in himself, his meaning songs convey'd
Informing morals to the shepherd maid ;   10
Or taught the swains that surest bliss to find,
What groves nor streams bestow, a virtuous mind.

When sweet and blushing, like a virgin bride,
The radiant Morn resum'd her orient pride ;
When wanton gales along the valleys play,   15
Breathe on each flow'r, and bear their sweets away ;
By Tigris' wand'ring waves he sate, and sung
This useful lesson for the fair and young.

"Ye Persian dames," he said, "to you belong,
Well may they please, the morals of my song :   20

8. No praise the youth, but hers alone desir'd :   — 1742.
13. When sweet and od'rous, like an Eastern bride,   — 1742.
17. By Tigris' wand'rer waves he sate, and sung   — 1742.
19. "Ye Persian dames," he said, "to ye belong,   — 1742.

No fairer maids, I trust, than you are found,
Grac'd with soft arts, the peopled world around !
The Morn that lights you, to your loves supplies
Each gentler ray delicious to your eyes :
For you those flow'rs her fragrant hands bestow,   25
And yours the love that kings delight to know.
Yet think not these, all beauteous as they are,
The best kind blessings heav'n can grant the fair !
Who trust alone in beauty's feeble ray,
Boast but the worth Balsora's [1] pearls display ;   30
Drawn from the deep we own their surface bright,
But, dark within, they drink no lustrous light :
Such are the maids, and such the charms they boast,
By sense unaided, or to virtue lost.
Self-flatt'ring sex ! your hearts believe in vain   35
That Love shall blind, when once he fires, the swain ;
Or hope a lover by your faults to win,
As spots on ermin beautify the skin :
Who seeks secure to rule, be first her care
Each softer virtue that adorns the fair ;   40
Each tender passion man delights to find,
The lov'd perfections of a female mind !

" Blest were the days when Wisdom held her reign,
And shepherds sought her on the silent plain ;
With Truth she wedded in the secret grove,   45
Immortal Truth, and daughters bless'd their love.

21. No fairer maids, I trust, than ye are found,   — 1742.
25. For ye those flow'rs her fragrant hands bestow,   — 1742.
30–32. Balsora's pearls have more of worth, than they ;
        Drawn from the deep, they sparkle to the sight,
        And all-unconscious shoot a lustrous light :   — 1742.
46. The fair-ey'd Truth, and daughters bless'd their love.
                                                          — 1742.

[1] The gulph of that name, famous for the pearl fishery. — C.

O haste, fair maids ! ye Virtues, come away !
Sweet Peace and Plenty lead you on your way !
The balmy shrub, for you, shall love our shore,
By Ind excell'd or Araby no more.   50

    " Lost to our fields, for so the Fates ordain,
The dear deserters shall return again.
Come thou, whose thoughts as limpid springs are clear,
To lead the train ; sweet Modesty, appear :
Here make thy court amidst our rural scene,   55
And shepherd girls shall own thee for their queen.
With thee be Chastity, of all afraid,
Distrusting all, a wise suspicious maid ;
But man the most—not more the mountain doe
Holds the swift falcon for her deadly foe.   60
Cold is her breast, like flow'rs that drink the dew ;
A silken veil conceals her from the view.
No wild Desires amidst thy train be known,
But Faith, whose heart is fix'd on one alone ;
Desponding Meekness with her down-cast eyes ;   65
And friendly Pity full of tender sighs ;
And Love the last.   By these your hearts approve,
These are the virtues that must lead to love."

    Thus sung the swain ; and ancient legends say,
The maids of Bagdat verified the lay :   70
Dear to the plains, the Virtues came along,
The shepherds lov'd, and Selim bless'd his song.

THE END OF THE FIRST ECLOGUE.

49. The balmy shrub, for ye, shall love our shore,   — 1742.
53, 54. O come, thou Modesty, as they decree,
    The rose may then improve her blush by thee. — 1742.
69. Thus sung the swain, and eastern legends say, — 1742.

ECLOGUE THE SECOND.

HASSAN ; OR, THE CAMEL DRIVER.

Scene, the desart.   *Time*, mid-day.

In silent horror o'er the boundless waste
The driver Hassan with his camels past.
One cruise of water on his back he bore,
And his light scrip contain'd a scanty store ;
A fan of painted feathers in his hand,   5
To guard his shaded face from scorching sand.
The sultry sun had gain'd the middle sky,
And not a tree, and not an herb was nigh ;
The beasts, with pain, their dusty way pursue,
Shrill roar'd the winds, and dreary was the view !   10
With desp'rate sorrow wild, th' affrighted man
Thrice sigh'd, thrice strook his breast, and thus began :
  "Sad was the hour, and luckless was the day,
  "When first from Schiraz' walls I bent my way.

  "Ah ! little thought I of the blasting wind,   15
The thirst or pinching hunger that I find !
Bethink thee, Hassan, where shall Thirst asswage,
When fails this cruise, his unrelenting rage?
Soon shall this scrip its precious load resign ;
Then what but tears and hunger shall be thine ?   20

  "Ye mute companions of my toils, that bear
In all my griefs a more than equal share !
Here, where no springs in murmurs break away,
Or moss-crown'd fountains mitigate the day,
In vain ye hope the green delights to know,   25
Which plains more blest, or verdant vales bestow :

---

1. In silent horror o'er the desart-waste
                                                    — 1742.

Here rocks alone, and tasteless sands, are found,
And faint and sickly winds forever howl around.
 " Sad was the hour, and luckless was the day,
 " When first from Schiraz' walls I bent my way! 30

 "Curst be the gold and silver which persuade
Weak men to follow far-fatiguing trade !
The lilly peace outshines the silver store,
And life is dearer than the golden ore:
Yet money tempts us o'er the desart brown, 35
To ev'ry distant mart and wealthy town.
Full oft we tempt the land, and oft the sea ;
And are we only yet repaid by thee ?
Ah ! why was ruin so attractive made,
Or why fond man so easily betrayed ? 40
Why heed we not, whilst mad we haste along,
The gentle voice of Peace, or Pleasure's song ?
Or wherefore think the flow'ry mountain's side,
The fountain's murmurs, and the valley's pride,
Why think we these less pleasing to behold, 45
Than dreary desarts if they lead to gold ?
 " Sad was the hour, and luckless was the day,
 " When first from Schiraz' walls I bent my way!

 " O cease, my fears !— all frantic as I go,
When thought creates unnumber'd scenes of woe, 50
What if the lion in his rage I meet !—
Oft in the dust I view his printed feet:
And (fearful !) oft, when Day's declining light
Yields her pale empire to the mourner Night,
By hunger rous'd, he scours the groaning plain, 55
Gaunt wolves and sullen tygers in his train:
Before them Death with shrieks directs their way,
Fills the wild yell, and leads them to their prey.

" Sad was the hour, and luckless was the day,
" When first from Schiraz' walls I bent my way !   60

" At that dead hour the silent asp shall creep,
If aught of rest I find, upon my sleep :
Or some swoln serpent twist his scales around,
And wake to anguish with a burning wound.
Thrice happy they, the wise contented poor,   65
From lust of wealth, and dread of death secure !
They tempt no desarts, and no griefs they find ;
Peace rules the day, where reason rules the mind.
" Sad was the hour, and luckless was the day,
" When first from Schiraz' walls I bent my way !   70

" O hapless youth ! for she thy love hath won,
The tender Zara, will be most undone !
Big swell'd my heart, and own'd the pow'rful maid,
When fast she dropp'd her tears, as thus she said :
' Farewell the youth whom sighs could not detain,   75
Whom Zara's breaking heart implor'd in vain !
Yet, as thou go'st, may ev'ry blast arise
Weak and unfelt as these rejected sighs !
Safe o'er the wild, no perils mayst thou see,
No griefs endure, nor weep, false youth, like me.'   80
O let me safely to the fair return,
Say with a kiss, she must not, shall not mourn !
O let me teach my heart to lose its fears,
Recall'd by Wisdom's voice, and Zara's tears ! "

He said, and call'd on heav'n to bless the day,   85
When back to Schiraz' walls he bent his way.

THE END OF THE SECOND ECLOGUE.

83. Go teach my heart to lose its painful fears,   — 1742.

ECLOGUE THE THIRD.

ABRA; OR, THE GEORGIAN SULTANA.

Scene, a forest.   *Time*, the evening.

In Georgia's land, where Tefflis' tow'rs are seen,
In distant view along the level green,
While ev'ning dews enrich the glitt'ring glade,
And the tall forests cast a longer shade,
What time 't is sweet o'er fields of rice to stray,   5
Or scent the breathing maize at setting day;[1]
Amidst the maids of Zagen's peaceful grove,
Emyra sung the pleasing cares of love.

Of Abra first began the tender strain,
Who led her youth with flocks upon the plain: 10
At morn she came those willing flocks to lead,
Where lillies rear them in the wat'ry mead;
From early dawn the live-long hours she told,
Till late at silent eve she penn'd the fold.
Deep in the grove, beneath the secret shade,   15
A various wreath of od'rous flow'rs she made:
Gay-motley'd pinks and sweet jonquils she chose,
The violet blue that on the moss-bank grows;
All sweet to sense, the flaunting rose was there:[2]
The finish'd chaplet well adorn'd her hair.   20

Great Abbas chanc'd that fated morn to stray,
By Love conducted from the chace away;
Among the vocal vales he heard her song,
And sought the vales and echoing groves among:

[1] Lines 5 and 6 were not in the edition of 1742.
[2] That these flowers are found in very great abundance in some of the provinces of Persia, see the *Modern History* of the ingenious Mr. Salmon. — C.

At length he found and woo'd the rural maid ;   25
She knew the monarch, and with fear obey'd.
    " Be ev'ry youth like royal Abbas mov'd,
    " And ev'ry Georgian maid like Abra lov'd ! "

    The royal lover bore her from the plain ;
Yet still her crook and bleating flock remain :   30
Oft, as she went, she backward turn'd her view,
And bad that crook and bleating flock adieu.
Fair happy maid ! to other scenes remove,
To richer scenes of golden power and love !
Go leave the simple pipe, and shepherd's strain ;   35
With love delight thee, and with Abbas reign.
    " Be ev'ry youth like royal Abbas mov'd,
    " And ev'ry Georgian maid like Abra lov'd ! "

    Yet midst the blaze of courts she fix'd her love
On the cool fountain, or the shady grove ;   40
Still with the shepherd's innocence her mind
To the sweet vale and flow'ry mead inclin'd ;
And oft as Spring renew'd the plains with flow'rs,
Breath'd his soft gales, and led the fragrant Hours,
With sure return she sought the sylvan scene,   45
The breezy mountains, and the forests green.
Her maids around her mov'd, a duteous band.
Each bore a crook, all rural, in her hand :
Some simple lay of flocks and herds they sung ;
With joy the mountain and the forest rung.   50
    " Be ev'ry youth like royal Abbas mov'd,
    " And ev'ry Georgian maid like Abra lov'd !

And oft the royal lover left the care
And thorns of state, attendant on the fair ;
Oft to the shades and low-roof'd cots retir'd,   55
Or sought the vale where first his heart was fir'd :

A russet mantle, like a swain, he wore,
And thought of crowns and busy courts no more.
 " Be ev'ry youth like royal Abbas mov'd,
 " And ev'ry Georgian maid like Abra lov'd ! " 60

Blest was the life that royal Abbas led :
Sweet was his love, and innocent his bed.
What if in wealth the noble maid excel ;
The simple shepherd girl can love as well.
Let those who rule on Persia's jewell'd throne, 65
Be fam'd for love, and gentlest love, alone ;
Or wreath, like Abbas, full of fair renown,
The lover's myrtle with the warrior's crown.
O happy days ! the maids around her say ;
O haste, profuse of blessings, haste away ! 70
 " Be ev'ry youth like royal Abbas mov'd,
 " And ev'ry Georgian maid like Abra lov'd ! "

THE END OF THE THIRD ECLOGUE.

ECLOGUE THE FOURTH.

AGIB AND SECANDER ; OR, THE FUGITIVES.

Scene, a mountain in Circassia. *Time,* midnight.

In fair Circassia, where, to love inclin'd,
Each swain was blest, for ev'ry maid was kind ;
At that still hour when awful midnight reigns,
And none but wretches haunt the twilight plains ;
What time the moon had hung her lamp on high, 5
And past in radiance thro' the cloudless sky ;
Sad, o'er the dews, two brother shepherds fled,
Where wild'ring Fear and desp'rate Sorrow led :

Fast as they prest their flight, behind them lay
Wide ravag'd plains, and vallies stole away.   10
Along the mountain's bending sides they ran,
Till, faint and weak, Secander thus began.

SECANDER.

O stay thee, Agib, for my feet deny,
No longer friendly to my life, to fly.
Friend of my heart, O turn thee and survey,   15
Trace our sad flight thro' all its length of way!
And first review that long extended plain,
And yon wide groves, already past with pain!
Yon ragged cliff, whose dang'rous path we try'd!
And last this lofty mountain's weary side!   20

AGIB.

Weak as thou art, yet hapless must thou know
The toils of flight, or some severer woe!
Still, as I haste, the Tartar shouts behind,
And shrieks and sorrows load the sadd'ning wind:
In rage of heart, with ruin in his hand,   25
He blasts our harvests, and deforms our land.
Yon citron grove, whence first in fear we came,
Droops its fair honours to the conqu'ring flame
Far fly the swains, like us, in deep despair,
And leave to ruffian bands their fleecy care.   30

SECANDER.

Unhappy land, whose blessings tempt the sword,
In vain, unheard, thou call'st thy Persian lord!
In vain thou court'st him, helpless, to thine aid
To shield the shepherd, and protect the maid!
Far off, in thoughtless indolence resign'd,   35
Soft dreams of love and pleasure sooth his mind:

Midst fair sultanas lost in idle joy,
No wars alarm him, and no fears annoy.

AGIB.

Yet these green hills, in summer's sultry heat,
Have lent the monarch oft a cool retreat.   40
Sweet to the sight is Zabran's flow'ry plain,
And once by maids and shepherds lov'd in vain !
No more the virgins shall delight to rove
By Sargis' banks, or Irwan's shady grove ;
On Tarkie's mountain catch the cooling gale,   45
Or breathe the scents of Aly's flow'ry vale :
Fair scenes ! but, ah ! no more with peace possest,
With ease alluring, and with plenty blest.
No more the shepherds' whit'ning tents appear,
Nor the kind products of a bounteous year ;   50
No more the date with snowy blossoms crown'd !
But Ruin spreads her baleful fires around.

SECANDER.

In vain Circassia boasts her spicy groves,
For ever fam'd for pure and happy loves :
In vain she boasts her fairest of the fair,   55
Their eyes' blue languish, and their golden hair !
Those eyes in tears their fruitless grief must send ;
Those hairs the Tartar's cruel hand shall rend.

AGIB.

Ye Georgian swains that piteous learn from far
Circassia's ruin, and the waste of war,   60
Some weightier arms than crooks and staves prepare,
To shield your harvests, and defend your fair :

49. No more the shepherds' whit'ning seats appear,   — 1742.
51. No more the dale with snowy blossoms crown'd !   — 1742.

The Turk and Tartar like designs pursue,
Fix'd to destroy, and steadfast to undo.
Wild as his land, in native desarts bred,   65
By lust incited, or by malice led,
The villain Arab, as he prowls for prey,
Oft marks with blood and wasting flames the way;
Yet none so cruel as the Tartar foe,
To death inur'd, and nurst in scenes of woe.   70

He said; when loud along the vale was heard
A shriller shriek, and nearer fires appear'd :
Th' affrighted shepherds, thro' the dews of night,
Wide o'er the moonlight hills renew'd their flight.

THE END OF THE FOURTH AND LAST ECLOGUE.

AN EPISTLE

ADDRESST TO SIR THOMAS HANMER ON HIS EDITION
OF SHAKESPEAR'S WORKS.

TO SIR THOMAS HANMER:

Sir,

While, born to bring the Muse's happier days,
A patriot's hand protects a poet's lays:
While, nurst by you, she sees her myrtles bloom,
Green and unwither'd o'er his honour'd tomb:
Excuse her doubts, if yet she fears to tell   5
What secret transports in her bosom swell:
With conscious awe she hears the critic's fame,
And blushing hides her wreath at Shakespear's name.
Hard was the lot those injur'd strains endur'd,
Unown'd by Science, and by years obscur'd: 10
Fair Fancy wept; and echoing sighs confest
A fixt despair in ev'ry tuneful breast.
Not with more grief th' afflicted swains appear
When wintry winds deform the plenteous year:

1-6. While, own'd by you, with smiles the Muse surveys
     Th' expected triumph of her sweetest lays;
     While, stretch'd at ease, she boasts your guardian aid,
     Secure and happy in her sylvan shade;
     Excuse her fears, who scarce a verse bestows
     In just remembrance of the debt she owes: — 1743.
9-16. Long-slighted Fancy, with a mother's care,
     Wept o'er his works, and felt the last despair.
     Torn from her head, she saw the roses fall,
     By all deserted, tho' admir'd by all.
     "And oh!" she cry'd, "shall Science still resign
     Whate'er is Nature's, and whate'er is mine?
     Shall Taste and Art but shew a cold regard,
     And scornful Pride reject th' unletter'd bard?
     Ye myrtled nymphs, who own my gentle reign,
     Tune the sweet lyre, and grace my airy train!

When ling'ring frosts the ruin'd seats invade   15
Where Peace resorted, and the Graces play'd.

Each rising art by just gradation moves,
Toil builds on toil, and age on age improves :
The Muse alone unequal dealt her rage,
And grac'd with noblest pomp her earliest stage.   20
Preserv'd thro' time, the speaking scenes impart
Each changeful wish of Phædra's tortur'd heart :
Or paint the curse that mark'd the Theban's [1] reign,
A bed incestuous, and a father slain.
With kind concern our pitying eyes o'erflow,   25
Trace the sad tale, and own another's woe.

To Rome remov'd, with wit secure to please,
The Comic Sisters kept their native ease.
With jealous fear declining Greece beheld
Her own Menander's art almost excell'd !   30
But ev'ry Muse essay'd to raise in vain
Some labour'd rival of her tragic strain ;
Ilissus' laurels, tho' transferr'd with toil,
Droop'd their fair leaves, nor knew th' unfriendly soil.

> If, where ye rove, your searching eyes have known
> One perfect mind, which judgment calls its own :
> There ev'ry breast its fondest hopes must bend,
> And ev'ry Muse with tears await her friend."
> 'T was then fair Isis from her stream arose,
> In kind compassion of her sister's woes.
> 'T was then she promis'd to the mourning maid
> Th' immortal honours, which thy hands have paid :
> " My best-lov'd son," she said, "shall yet restore
> Thy ruin'd sweets, and Fancy weep no more."   — 1743.
> 25. Line after line, our pitying eyes o'erflow,   — 1743.
> 27. To Rome remov'd, with equal pow'r to please,   — 1743.

[1] The *Œdipus* of Sophocles. — C.

As Arts expir'd, resistless Dullness rose ;　35
Goths, priests, or Vandals, — all were Learning's foes.
Till Julius [1] first recall'd each exil'd maid,
And Cosmo own'd them in th' Etrurian shade :
Then, deeply skill'd in love's engaging theme,
The soft Provençal pass'd to Arno's stream :　40
With graceful ease the wanton lyre he strung,
Sweet flow'd the lays — but love was all he sung.
The gay description could not fail to move ;
For, led by nature, all are friends to love.

But heav'n, still various in its works, decreed　45
The perfect boast of time should last succeed.
The beauteous union must appear, at length,
Of Tuscan fancy, and Athenian strength :
One greater Muse Eliza's reign adorn,
And ev'n a Shakespear to her fame be born !　50

Yet ah ! so bright her morning's op'ning ray,
In vain our Britain hop'd an equal day !
No second growth the western isle could bear,
At once exhausted with too rich a year.
Too nicely Johnson knew the critic's part ;　55
Nature in him was almost lost in art.

35–42.　When Rome herself, her envy'd glories dead,
　　　No more imperial, stoop'd her conquer'd head :
　　　Luxuriant Florence chose a softer theme,
　　　While all was peace, by Arno's silver stream.
　　　With sweeter notes th' Etrurian vales complain'd,
　　　And arts reviving told — a Cosmo reign'd.
　　　Their wanton lyres the bards of Provence strung,
　　　Sweet flow'd the lays, but love was all they sung.　— 1743.
　45.　But heav'n, still rising in its works, decreed　— 1743.

[1] Julius the Second, the immediate predecessor of Leo the Tenth. — C.

Of softer mold the gentle Fletcher came,
The next in order, as the next in name.
With pleas'd attention midst his scenes we find
Each glowing thought that warms the female mind ;   60
Each melting sigh, and ev'ry tender tear,
The lover's wishes and the virgin's fear.
His ev'ry strain the Smiles and Graces own;[1]
But stronger Shakespear felt for man alone :
Drawn by his pen, our ruder passions stand   65
Th' unrivall'd picture of his early hand.

With gradual steps and slow,[2] exacter France
Saw Art's fair empire o'er her shores advance :
By length of toil, a bright perfection knew,
Correctly bold, and just in all she drew.   70
Till late Corneille, with Lucan's[3] spirit fir'd,
Breath'd the free strain, as Rome and he inspir'd :
And classic judgment gained to sweet Racine
The temp'rate strength of Maro's chaster line.

But wilder far the British laurel spread,   75
And wreaths less artful crown our poet's head.
Yet he alone to ev'ry scene could give
Th' historian's truth, and bid the manners live.
Wak'd at his call I view, with glad surprise,
Majestic forms of mighty monarchs rise.   80

---

63. His ev'ry strain the Loves and Graces own ;   — 1743.
71, 72. Till late Corneille from epick Lucan brought
        The full expression, and the Roman thought ;   — 1743.

[1] Their characters are thus distinguished by Mr. Dryden. — C.

[2] About the time of Shakespear, the poet Hardy was in great repute in France.   He wrote, according to Fontenelle, six hundred plays. The French poets after him applied themselves in general to the correct improvement of the stage, which was almost totally disregarded by those of our own country, Johnson excepted. — C.

[3] The favourite author of the elder Corneille. — C.

There Henry's trumpets spread their loud alarms,
And laurell'd Conquest waits her hero's arms.
Here gentler Edward claims a pitying sigh,
Scarce born to honours, and so soon to die!
Yet shall thy throne, unháppy infant, bring   85
No beam of comfort to the guilty king:
The time shall come[1] when Glo'ster's heart shall bleed,
In life's last hours, with horror of the deed:
When dreary visions shall at last present
Thy vengeful image, in the midnight tent: 90
Thy hand unseen the secret death shall bear,
Blunt the weak sword, and break th' oppressive spear.

Where'er we turn, by Fancy charm'd, we find
Some sweet illusion of the cheated mind.
Oft, wild of wing, she calls the soul to rove   95
With humbler nature, in the rural grove;
Where swains contented own the quiet scene,
And twilight fairies tread the circled green:
Drest by her hand, the woods and vallies smile,
And Spring diffusive decks th' enchanted isle.   100

O more than all in pow'rful genius blest,
Come, take thine empire o'er the willing breast!
Whate'er the wounds this youthful heart shall feel,
Thy songs support me, and thy morals heal!
There ev'ry thought the poet's warmth may raise,   105
There native music dwells in all the lays.

101–110.   O blest in all that genius gives to charm,
            Whose morals mend us, and whose passions warm!
            Oft let my youth attend thy various page,
            Where rich invention rules th' unbounded stage.

[1] Tempus erit Turno, magno cum optaverit emptum
     Intactum Pallanta, etc.   VIRG. — C.

O might some verse with happiest skill persuade
Expressive Picture to adopt thine aid,
What wondrous draughts might rise from ev'ry page,
What other Raphaels charm a distant age!   110
Methinks ev'n now I view some free design,
Where breathing nature lives in ev'ry line :
Chaste and subdu'd the modest lights decay,
Steal into shade, and mildly melt away.
— And see, where Anthony,[1] in tears approv'd,   115
Guards the pale relicks of the chief he lov'd :
O'er the cold corse the warrior seems to bend,
Deep sunk in grief, and mourns his murther'd friend !
Still as they press, he calls on all around,
Lifts the torn robe, and points the bleeding wound.   120

But who is he,[2] whose brows exalted bear
A wrath impatient, and a fiercer air ?
Awake to all that injur'd worth can feel,
On his own Rome he turns th' avenging steel.

There ev'ry scene the poet's warmth may raise,
And melting music find the softest lays.
O might the Muse with equal ease persuade
Expressive Picture to adopt thine aid,
Some pow'rful Raphael should again appear,
And Arts consenting fix their empire here.   — 1743.
111. Methinks ev'n now I view some fair design,   — 1743.
113–116. Chaste, and subdu'd, the modest colours lie,
In fair proportion to th' approving eye.
And see, where Antony lamenting stands
In fix'd distress, and spreads his pleading hands !
          — 1743.
122–124. A rage impatient, and a fiercer air ?
Ev'n now his thoughts with eager vengeance doom
The last sad ruin of ungrateful Rome.
          — 1743.

[1] See the tragedy of *Julius Caesar.* — C.
[2] Coriolanus. See Mr. Spence's *Dialogues on the Odyssey.* — C.

Yet shall not War's insatiate fury fall   125
(So heav'n ordains it) on the destin'd wall.
See the fond mother, midst the plaintive train,
Hung on his knees, and prostrate on the plain!
Touch'd to the soul, in vain he strives to hide
The son's affection, in the Roman's pride :   130
O'er all the man conflicting passions rise,
Rage grasps the sword, while Pity melts the eyes.

   Thus, gen'rous critic, as thy bard inspires,
The sister Arts shall nurse their drooping fires ;
Each from his scenes her stores alternate bring,   135
Blend the fair tints, or wake the vocal string :
Those sibyl-leaves, the sport of ev'ry wind
(For poets ever were a careless kind),
By thee dispos'd, no farther toil demand,
But, just to nature, own thy forming hand.   140

   So, spread o'er Greece, th' harmonious whole unknown,
Ev'n Homer's numbers charm'd by parts alone.
Their own Ulysses scarce had wander'd more,
By winds and waters[1] cast on ev'ry shore :
When, rais'd by fate, some former Hanmer joined   145
Each beauteous image of the boundless mind :
And bad, like thee, his Athens ever claim
A fond alliance with the poet's name.

125-130. Till, slow-advancing o'er the tented plain,
              In sable weeds, appear the kindred-train :
              The frantic mother leads their wild despair,
              Beats her swoln breast, and rends her silver hair.
              And see, he yields ! the tears unbidden start,
              And conscious nature claims th' unwilling heart ! — 1743.
   136. Spread the fair tints, or wake the vocal string :   — 1743.
   146. Each beauteous image of the tuneful mind ;   — 1743.

[1] In the edition of 1744, the reading is *water ;* but as this seems
like a mere typographical error, the earlier text has been followed.

ODES

ON SEVERAL DESCRIPTIVE AND ALLEGORIC SUBJECTS.

—— Εἴην
Εὑρησιεπὴς ἀναγεῖσθαι
Πρόσφορος ἐν Μοισᾶν Δίφρῳ·
Τόλμα δὲ καὶ ἀμφιλαφὴς δύναμις
Ἕσποιτο. ——
— Πινδαρ. Ολυμπ. θ.

ODE TO PITY.

O THOU, the friend of man, assign'd
With balmy hands his wounds to bind,
   And charm his frantic woe :
When first Distress with dagger keen
Broke forth to waste his destin'd scene,   5
   His wild unsated foe !

By Pella's bard,[1] a magic name,
By all the griefs his thought could frame,
   Receive my humble rite :
Long, Pity, let the nations view   10
Thy sky-worn robes of tend'rest blue,
   And eyes of dewy light !

But wherefore need I wander wide
To old Ilissus' distant side,
   Deserted stream, and mute ?   15
Wild Arun[2] too has heard thy strains,
And Echo, midst my native plains,
   Been sooth'd by Pity's lute.

There first the wren thy myrtles shed
On gentlest Otway's infant head,   20
   To him thy cell was shown ;
And while he sung the female heart,
With youth's soft notes unspoil'd by art,
   Thy turtles mix'd their own.

---

[1] Euripides, of whom Aristotle pronounces, on a comparison of
him with Sophocles, that he was the greater master of the tender
passions, ἦν τραγικώτερος. — C.

[2] The river Arun runs by the village in Sussex, where Otway had
his birth. — C.

Come, Pity, come! By Fancy's aid,   25
Ev'n now my thoughts, relenting maid,
    Thy temple's pride design:
Its southern site, its truth compleat,
Shall raise a wild enthusiast heat
    In all who view the shrine.   30

There Picture's toils shall well relate
How chance, or hard involving fate,
    O'er mortal bliss prevail:
The buskin'd Muse shall near her stand,
And sighing prompt her tender hand   35
    With each disastrous tale.

There let me oft, retir'd by day,
In dreams of passion melt away,
    Allow'd with thee to dwell:
There waste the mournful lamp of night,   40
Till, virgin, thou again delight
    To hear a British shell!

ODE TO FEAR.

STROPHE.

THOU to whom the world unknown
With all its shadowy shapes is shown;
Who see'st appall'd th' unreal scene,
While Fancy lifts the veil between:
    Ah Fear! ah frantic Fear!   5
    I see, I see thee near!
I know thy hurried step, thy haggard eye!
Like thee I start, like thee disorder'd fly,
For lo what monsters in thy train appear!

Danger, whose limbs of giant mold　　　10
What mortal eye can fix'd behold?
Who stalks his round, an hideous form,
Howling amidst the midnight storm,
Or throws him on the ridgy steep
Of some loose hanging rock to sleep:　　　15
And with him thousand phantoms join'd,
Who prompt to deeds accurs'd the mind:
And those, the fiends who, near allied,
O'er Nature's wounds and wrecks preside;
Whilst Vengeance, in the lurid air,　　　20
Lifts her red arm, expos'd and bare:
On whom that rav'ning brood of Fate,[1]
Who lap the blood of Sorrow, wait;
Who, Fear, this ghastly train can see,
And look not madly wild, like thee?　　　25

EPODE.

In earliest Greece to thee, with partial choice,
　　The grief-full Muse addrest her infant tongue;
The maids and matrons, on her awful voice,
　　Silent and pale in wild amazement hung.

Yet he, the bard[2] who first invok'd thy name,　　　30
　　Disdain'd in Marathon its pow'r to feel:
For not alone he nurs'd the poet's flame,
　　But reach'd from Virtue's hand the patriot's steel.

But who is he whom later garlands grace,
　　Who left awhile o'er Hybla's dews to rove,　　　35
With trembling eyes thy dreary steps to trace,
　　Where thou and Furies shar'd the baleful grove?

---

[1] Alluding to the κύνας ἀφύκτους of Sophocles. See the *Electra.* — C.
[2] Æschylus. — C.

Wrapt in thy cloudy veil th' incestuous queen [1]
   Sigh'd the sad call [2] her son and husband heard,
When once alone it broke the silent scene,   40
   And he, the wretch of Thebes, no more appear'd.

O Fear, I know thee by my throbbing heart:
   Thy with'ring pow'r inspir'd each mournful line ;
Tho' gentle Pity claim her mingled part,
   Yet all the thunders of the scene are thine !   45

ANTISTROPHE.

Thou who such weary lengths hast past,
Where wilt thou rest, mad nymph, at last?
Say, wilt thou shroud in haunted cell,
Where gloomy Rape and Murder dwell?
   Or in some hollow'd seat,   50
   'Gainst which the big waves beat,
Hear drowning seamen's cries in tempests brought?
Dark pow'r, with shudd'ring, meek, submitted thought
Be mine to read the visions old
Which thy awak'ning bards have told :   55
And, lest thou meet my blasted view,
Hold each strange tale devoutly true ;
Ne'er be I found, by thee o'eraw'd,
In that thrice-hallow'd eve abroad
When ghosts, as cottage maids believe,   60
Their pebbled beds permitted leave,
And goblins haunt, from fire, or fen,
Or mine, or flood, the walks of men !

[1] Jocasta. — C.
[2]
      —— οὐδ' ἔτ' ὡρώρει βοή,
    Ἧν μὲν σιωπή ; φθέγμα δ' ἐξαίφνης τινὸς
    θώΰξεν αὐτόν, ὥστε πάντας ὀρθίας
    Στῆσαι φόβῳ δείσαντας ἐξαίφνης τρίχας.
    See the *Œdip. Colon.* of Sophocles. — C.

O thou whose spirit most possest
The sacred seat of Shakespear's breast,   65
By all that from thy prophet broke,
In thy divine emotions spoke,
Hither again thy fury deal !
Teach me but once like him to feel,
His cypress wreath my meed decree,   70
And I, O Fear, will dwell with thee !

ODE TO SIMPLICITY.

O THOU by Nature taught
To breathe her genuine thought,
In numbers warmly pure, and sweetly strong :
    Who first, on mountains wild,
    In Fancy, loveliest child,   5
Thy babe or Pleasure's, nurs'd the pow'rs of song !

Thou who with hermit heart
Disdain'st the wealth of art,
And gauds, and pageant weeds, and trailing pall,
    But com'st a decent maid   10
    In Attic robe array'd,
O chaste, unboastful nymph, to thee I call !

By all the honey'd store
On Hybla's thymy shore,
By all her blooms, and mingled murmurs dear,   15
    By her [1] whose lovelorn woe
    In ev'ning musings slow
Sooth'd sweetly sad Electra's poet's ear :

---

[1] The ἀηδών, or nightingale, for which Sophocles seems to have
entertain'd a peculiar fondness. — C.

By old Cephisus deep,
Who spread his wavy sweep   20
In warbled wand'rings round thy green retreat,
    On whose enamell'd side
    When holy Freedom died,
No equal haunt allur'd thy future feet:

O sister meek of Truth,   25
    To my admiring youth
Thy sober aid and native charms infuse !
    The flow'rs that sweetest breathe,
    Tho' Beauty cull'd the wreath,
Still ask thy hand to range their order'd hues.   30

While Rome could none esteem
    But virtue's patriot theme,
You lov'd her hills, and led her laureate band :
    But staid to sing alone
    To one distinguish'd throne,   35
And turn'd thy face, and fled her alter'd land.

No more, in hall or bow'r,
    The passions own thy pow'r ;
Love, only love, her forceless numbers mean :
    For thou hast left her shrine ;   40
    Nor olive more, nor vine,
Shall gain thy feet to bless the servile scene.

Tho' taste, tho' genius bless
    To some divine excess,
Faints the cold work till thou inspire the whole ;   45
    What each, what all supply,
    May court, may charm our eye,
Thou, only thou, canst raise the meeting soul !

Of these let others ask,
　　To aid some mighty task ;　　　　　　50
I only seek to find thy temp'rate vale :
　　Where oft my reed might sound
　　To maids and shepherds round,
And all thy sons, O Nature, learn my tale.

ODE ON THE POETICAL CHARACTER.

STROPHE.

As once, if not with light regard
I read aright that gifted bard
(Him whose school above the rest
His loveliest Elfin Queen has blest),
One, only one, unrivall'd fair [1]　　　　　5
Might hope the magic girdle wear,
At solemn turney hung on high,
The wish of each love-darting eye ;
Lo ! to each other nymph in turn applied,
　　As if, in air unseen, some hov'ring hand,　　10
Some chaste and angel friend to virgin fame,
　　With whisper'd spell had burst the starting band,
It left unblest her loath'd, dishonour'd side ;
　　Happier hopeless fair, if never
　　Her baffled hand with vain endeavour　　　15
Had touch'd that fatal zone to her denied !
Young Fancy thus, to me divinest name,
　　To whom, prepar'd and bath'd in heav'n,
　　The cest of amplest pow'r is giv'n,
　　To few the godlike gift assigns,　　　　20
　　To gird their blest, prophetic loins,
And gaze her visions wild, and feel unmix'd her flame !

[1] Florimel.　See Spenser, Leg. 4th. — C.

EPODE.

The band, as fairy legends say,
Was wove on that creating day
When He who call'd with thought to birth   25
Yon tented sky, this laughing earth,
And drest with springs and forests tall,
And pour'd the main engirting all,
Long by the lov'd enthusiast woo'd,
Himself in some diviner mood,   30
Retiring, sate with her alone,
And plac'd her on his sapphire throne,
The whiles, the vaulted shrine around,
Seraphic wires were heard to sound,
Now sublimest triumph swelling,   35
Now on love and mercy dwelling;
And she, from out the veiling cloud,
Breath'd her magic notes aloud:
And thou, thou rich-hair'd Youth of Morn,
And all thy subject life, was born!   40
The dang'rous Passions kept aloof,
Far from the sainted growing woof:
But near it sate ecstatic Wonder,
List'ning the deep applauding thunder;
And Truth, in sunny vest array'd,   45
By whose the tarsel's eyes were made;
All the shad'wy tribes of mind
In braided dance their murmurs join'd,
And all the bright uncounted Pow'rs
Who feed on heav'n's ambrosial flow'rs.   50
Where is the bard whose soul can now
Its high presuming hopes avow?
Where he who thinks, with rapture blind,
This hallow'd work for him design'd?

ANTISTROPHE.

High on some cliff, to heav'n up-pil'd,   55
Of rude access, of prospect wild,
Where, tangled round the jealous steep,
Strange shades o'er-brow the valleys deep,
And holy genii guard the rock,
Its glooms embrown, its springs unlock,   60
While on its rich ambitious head
An Eden, like his own, lies spread,
I view that oak, the fancied glades among,
By which as Milton lay, his ev'ning ear,
From many a cloud that dropp'd ethereal dew,   65
Nigh spher'd in heav'n its native strains could hear,
On which that ancient trump he reach'd was hung :
   Thither oft, his glory greeting,
   From Waller's myrtle shades retreating,
With many a vow from Hope's aspiring tongue,   70
My trembling feet his guiding steps pursue ;
   In vain — such bliss to one alone
   Of all the sons of soul was known,
   And Heav'n and Fancy, kindred pow'rs,
   Have now o'erturn'd th' inspiring bow'rs,   75
Or curtain'd close such scene from ev'ry future view.

ODE

WRITTEN IN THE BEGINNING OF THE YEAR 1746.

How sleep the brave who sink to rest
By all their country's wishes blest!
When Spring, with dewy fingers cold,
Returns to deck their hallow'd mold,

She there shall dress a sweeter sod
Than Fancy's feet have ever trod.

By fairy hands their knell is rung,
By forms unseen their dirge is sung;
There Honour comes, a pilgrim grey,
To bless the turf that wraps their clay;
And Freedom shall awhile repair,
To dwell a weeping hermit there!

ODE TO MERCY.

STROPHE.

O THOU who sitt'st a smiling bride
By Valour's arm'd and awful side,
Gentlest of sky-born forms, and best ador'd:
  Who oft with songs, divine to hear,
  Winn'st from his fatal grasp the spear,
And hid'st in wreaths of flow'rs his bloodless sword!
  Thou who, amidst the deathful field,
  By godlike chiefs alone beheld,
Oft with thy bosom bare art found,
Pleading for him the youth who sinks to ground:
  See, Mercy, see! with pure and loaded hands,
  Before thy shrine my country's genius stands,
And decks thy altar still, tho' pierc'd with many a wound!

ANTISTROPHE.

When he whom ev'n our joys provoke,
  The Fiend of Nature, join'd his yoke,
And rush'd in wrath to make our isle his prey,
  Thy form, from out thy sweet abode,
  O'ertook him on his blasted road,
And stopp'd his wheels, and look'd his rage away.

I see recoil his sable steeds, 20
That bore him swift to salvage deeds ;
Thy tender melting eyes they own.
O maid, for all thy love to Britain shown,
Where Justice bars her iron tow'r,
To thee we build a roseate bow'r. 25
Thou, thou shalt rule our queen, and share our monarch's
throne !

ODE TO LIBERTY.

STROPHE.

WHO shall awake the Spartan fife,
And call in solemn sounds to life
The youths whose locks divinely spreading,
Like vernal hyacinths in sullen hue,
At once the breath of fear and virtue shedding, 5
Applauding Freedom lov'd of old to view?
What new Alcæus,[1] fancy-blest,
Shall sing the sword, in myrtles drest,
At Wisdom's shrine awhile its flame concealing
(What place so fit to seal a deed renowned ?), 10
Till she her brightest lightnings round revealing,
It leap'd in glory forth, and dealt her prompted wound?

[1] Alluding to that beautiful fragment of Alcæus :

Ἐν μύρτου κλαδὶ τὸ ξίφος φορήσω,
Ὥσπερ Ἁρμόδιος κ' Ἀριστογείτων,
Φίλταθ' Ἁρμόδι', οὔπω τέθνηκας,
Νήσοις δ' ἐν μακάρων σέ φασιν εἶναι·
Ἐν μύρτου κλαδὶ τὸ ξίφος φορήσω,
Ὥσπερ Ἁρμόδιος κ' Ἀριστογείτων,
Ὅτ' Ἀθηναίης ἐν θυσίαις,
Ἄνδρα τύραννον Ἵππαρχον ἐκαινέτην.
Ἀεὶ σφῷν κλέος ἔσσεται κατ' αἶαν,
Φίλταθ' Ἁρμόδι', κ' Ἀριστογείτων. — C.

O goddess, in that feeling hour,
When most its sounds would court thy ears,
   Let not my shell's misguided pow'r   15
E'er draw thy sad, thy mindful tears.[1]
No, Freedom, no, I will not tell
How Rome, before thy weeping face,
With heaviest sound, a giant statue, fell,
Push'd by a wild and artless race   20
From off its wide ambitious base,
When Time his Northern sons of spoil awoke,
   And all the blended work of strength and grace,
   With many a rude repeated stroke,
And many a barb'rous yell, to thousand fragments broke. 25

EPODE.

Yet ev'n where'er the least appear'd,
Th' admiring world thy hand rever'd ;
Still, midst the scatter'd states around,
Some remnants of her strength were found ;
They saw, by what escap'd the storm,   30
How wondrous rose her perfect form,
How in the great, the labour'd whole,
Each mighty master pour'd his soul !
For sunny Florence, seat of Art,
Beneath her vines preserv'd a part,   35
Till they[2] whom Science lov'd to name
(O who could fear it?) quench'd her flame.
And lo, an humbler relick laid
In jealous Pisa's olive shade !

---

[1] Μὴ μὴ ταῦτα λέγωμες, ἃ δάκρυον ἤγαγε Δηοῖ.
               — Callimach., "Ὕμνος εἰς Δήμητρα. — C.
[2] The family of the Medici. — C.

See, small Marino [1] joins the theme,   40
Tho' least, not last in thy esteem.
Strike, louder strike th' ennobling strings
To those [2] whose merchant sons were kings ;
To him [3] who, deck'd with pearly pride,
In Adria weds his green-hair'd bride.   45
Hail, port of glory, wealth, and pleasure !
Ne'er let me change this Lydian measure,
Nor e'er her former pride relate
To sad Liguria's [4] bleeding state.
Ah no ! more pleas'd thy haunts I seek,   50
On wild Helvetia's [5] mountains bleak
(Where, when the favor'd of thy choice,
The daring archer, heard thy voice,
Forth from his eyrie rous'd in dread,
The rav'ning eagle northward fled) :   55
Or dwell in willow'd meads more near,
With those [6] to whom thy stork is dear ;
Those whom the rod of Alva bruis'd,
Whose crown a British queen [7] refus'd !
The magic works, thou feel'st the strains,   60
One holier name alone remains ;
The perfect spell shall then avail :
Hail nymph, ador'd by Britain, hail !

---

[1] The little republic of San Marino. — C.
[2] The Venetians. — C.
[3] The Doge of Venice. — C.
[4] Genoa. — C.
[5] Switzerland. — C.
[6] The Dutch, amongst whom there are very severe penalties for
those who are convicted of killing this bird. They are kept tame
in almost all their towns, and particularly at the Hague, of the arms
of which they make a part. The common people of Holland are
said to entertain a superstitious sentiment, that if the whole species
of them should become extinct, they should lose their liberties. — C.
[7] Queen Elizabeth. — C.

ANTISTROPHE.

Beyond the measure vast of thought,
The works the wizard Time has wrought !   65
  The Gaul, 't is held of antique story,
Saw Britain link'd to his now adverse strand ; [1]
  No sea between, nor cliff sublime and hoary,
He pass'd with unwet feet thro' all our land.
    To the blown Baltic then, they say,   70
    The wild waves found another way,
Where Orcas howls, his wolfish mountains rounding ;
  Till all the banded West at once 'gan rise,
A wide wild storm ev'n Nature's self confounding,
  With'ring her giant sons with strange uncouth surprise. 75
    This pillar'd earth so firm and wide,
      By winds and inward labors torn,
    In thunders dread was push'd aside,
      And down the should'ring billows borne.
And see, like gems, her laughing train,   80
  The little isles on ev'ry side !
Mona, once hid from those who search the main,[2]

---

[1] This tradition is mentioned by several of our old historians.
Some naturalists, too, have endeavor'd to support the probability of
the fact, by arguments drawn from the correspondent disposition of
the two opposite coasts. I don't remember that any poetical use
has been hitherto made of it. — C.

[2] There is a tradition in the Isle of Man, that a mermaid, becoming
enamour'd of a young man of extraordinary beauty, took an opportunity of meeting him one day as he walk'd on the shore, and
open'd her passion to him, but was receiv'd with a coldness, occasion'd by his horror and surprise at her appearance. This, however,
was so misconstru'd by the sea-lady that, in revenge for his treatment of her, she punish'd the whole island by covering it with a
mist, so that all who attempted to carry on any commerce with it
either never arriv'd at it, but wander'd up and down the sea, or
were on a sudden wreck'd upon its cliffs. — C.

Where thousand elfin shapes abide,
And Wight, who checks the west'ring tide ;
 For thee consenting Heav'n has each bestowed,   85
A fair attendant on her sov'reign pride.
 To thee this blest divorce she ow'd,
For thou hast made her vales thy lov'd, thy last abode !

SECOND EPODE.

 Then too, 't is said, an hoary pile,
 Midst the green navel of our isle,   90
 Thy shrine in some religious wood,
 O soul-enforcing goddess, stood !
 There oft the painted native's feet
 Were wont thy form celestial meet :
 Tho' now with hopeless toil we trace   95
 Time's backward rolls to find its place ;
 Whether the fiery-tressed Dane
 Or Roman's self o'erturn'd the fane,
 Or in what heaven-left age it fell,
 'T were hard for modern song to tell.   100
 Yet still, if truth those beams infuse
 Which guide at once and charm the Muse,
 Beyond yon braided clouds that lie,
 Paving the light-embroider'd sky,
 Amidst the bright pavilion'd plains,   105
 The beauteous model still remains.
 There, happier than in islands blest,
 Or bow'rs by Spring or Hebe drest,
 The chiefs who fill our Albion's story,
 In warlike weeds, retir'd in glory,   110
 Hear their consorted druids sing
 Their triumphs to th' immortal string.
  How may the poet now unfold
 What never tongue or numbers told ?

How learn, delighted and amaz'd,   115
What hands unknown that fabric rais'd?
Ev'n now, before his favor'd eyes,
In Gothic pride it seems to rise!
Yet Græcia's graceful orders join,
Majestic thro' the mix'd design;   120
The secret builder knew to chuse
Each sphere-found gem of richest hues:
Whate'er heav'n's purer mold contains,
When nearer suns emblaze its veins;
There on the walls the patriot's sight   125
May ever hang with fresh delight,
And, grav'd with some prophetic rage,
Read Albion's fame thro' ev'ry age.

Ye forms divine, ye laureate band,
That near her inmost altar stand,   130
Now sooth her to her blissful train
Blithe Concord's social form to gain:
Concord, whose myrtle wand can steep
Ev'n Anger's bloodshot eyes in sleep:
Before whose breathing bosom's balm   135
Rage drops his steel, and storms grow calm.
Her let our sires and matrons hoar
Welcome to Britain's ravag'd shore;
Our youths, enamour'd of the fair,
Play with the tangles of her hair;   140
Till, in one loud applauding sound,
The nations shout to her around,
"O how supremely art thou blest!
Thou, lady, thou shalt rule the West!"

ODE TO A LADY

ON THE DEATH OF COLONEL ROSS IN THE ACTION OF FONTENOY.

WHILE, lost to all his former mirth,
Britannia's genius bends to earth,
   And mourns the fatal day :
While, stain'd with blood, he strives to tear
Unseemly from his sea-green hair   5
   The wreaths of chearful May :

The thoughts which musing Pity pays,
And fond Remembrance loves to raise,
   Your faithful hours attend :
Still Fancy, to herself unkind,   10
Awakes to grief the soften'd mind,
   And points the bleeding friend.

By rapid Scheld's descending wave
His country's vows shall bless the grave,
   Where'er the youth is laid :   15
That sacred spot the village hind
With ev'ry sweetest turf shall bind,
   And Peace protect the shade.

O'er him whose doom thy virtues grieve
Aerial forms shall sit at eve   20
   And bend the pensive head !
And, fall'n to save his injur'd land,
Imperial Honour's awful hand
   Shall point his lonely bed !

4. While, sunk in grief, he strives to tear   —MS.
19–24. Ev'n now, regardful of his doom,
    Applauding Honour haunts his tomb,
      With shadowy trophies crown'd :

The warlike dead of ev'ry age,   25
Who fill the fair recording page,
    Shall leave their sainted rest :
And, half-reclining on his spear,
Each wond'ring chief by turns appear,
    To hail the blooming guest.   30

Old Edward's sons, unknown to yield,
Shall crowd from Cressy's laurell'd field,
    And gaze with fix'd delight :
Again for Britain's wrongs they feel,
Again they snatch the gleamy steel,   35
    And wish th' avenging fight.[1]

    Whilst Freedom's form beside her roves
    Majestic thro' the twilight groves,
        And calls her heroes round.   — 1746.

    Blest youth, regardful of thy doom,
    Aerial hands shall build thy tomb,
        With shadowy trophies crown'd :
    Whilst Honour bathed in tears shall rove
    To sigh thy name thro' ev'ry grove,
        And call his heroes round.   — 1747.
    31. Old Edward's sons, untaught to yield,   — MS.

[1] In the text of 1747, the following stanzas were inserted after
line 36 :
            But lo where, sunk in deep despair,
            Her garments torn, her bosom bare,
                Impatient Freedom lies !
            Her matted tresses madly spread,
            To ev'ry sod which wraps the dead
                She turns her joyless eyes.

            Ne'er shall she leave that lowly ground,
            Till notes of triumph bursting round
                Proclaim her reign restor'd :
            Till William seek the sad retreat,
            And, bleeding at her sacred feet,
                Present the sated sword.

If, weak to sooth so soft an heart,
These pictur'd glories nought impart
   To dry thy constant tear :
If yet, in Sorrow's distant eye,   40
Expos'd and pale thou see'st him lie,
   Wild War insulting near :

Where'er from time thou court'st relief,
The Muse shall still, with social grief,
   Her gentlest promise keep :   45
Ev'n humble Harting's cottag'd vale
Shall learn the sad-repeated tale,
   And bid her shepherds weep.

ODE TO EVENING.

IF ought of oaten stop, or pastoral song,
May hope, chaste Eve, to sooth thy modest ear,
   Like thy own solemn springs,
   Thy springs and dying gales,

O nymph reserv'd, while now the bright-hair'd sun   5
Sits in yon western tent, whose cloudy skirts,
   With brede ethereal wove,
   O'erhang his wavy bed :

Now air is hush'd, save where the weak-ey'd bat,
With short shrill shriek, flits by on leathern wing,   10
   Or where the beetle winds
   His small but sullen horn,

37. If, drawn by all a lover's art,   — MS.
46. Ev'n humble Harting's cottage vale   — 1748.
47. Shall learn the sad repeated tale,   — 1747.
2, 3. May hope, O pensive Eve, to sooth thine ear,
      Like thy own brawling springs,   — 1747.

As oft he rises 'midst the twilight path,
Against the pilgrim borne in heedless hum :
   Now teach me, maid compos'd,   15
   To breathe some soften'd strain,

Whose numbers, stealing thro' thy dark'ning vale,
May not unseemly with its stillness suit,
   As, musing slow, I hail
   Thy genial lov'd return !   20

For when thy folding-star arising shews
His paly circlet, at his warning lamp
   The fragrant Hours, and elves
   Who slept in flow'rs the day,

And many a nymph who wreaths her brows with sedge, 25
And sheds the fresh'ning dew, and, lovelier still,
   The pensive Pleasures sweet,
   Prepare thy shadowy car.

Then lead, calm vot'ress, where some sheety lake
Cheers the lone heath, or some time-hallow'd pile   30
   Or upland fallows grey
   Reflect its last cool gleam.

But when chill blust'ring winds, or driving rain,
Forbid my willing feet, be mine the hut
   That from the mountain's side   35
   Views wilds, and swelling floods,

24. Who slept in buds the day,   — 1747.
29–32. Then let me rove some wild and heathy scene,
      Or find some ruin midst its dreary dells,
        Whose walls more awful nod
        By thy religious gleams.   — 1747.
33, 34. Or if chill blust'ring winds, or driving rain,
      Prevent my willing feet, be mine the hut   — 1747.

And hamlets brown, and dim-discover'd spires,
And hears their simple bell, and marks o'er all
   Thy dewy fingers draw
    The gradual dusky veil.   40

While Spring shall pour his show'rs, as oft he wont,
And bathe thy breathing tresses, meekest Eve;
   While Summer loves to sport
    Beneath thy ling'ring light;

While sallow Autumn fills thy lap with leaves;   45
Or Winter, yelling thro' the troublous air,
   Affrights thy shrinking train,
    And rudely rends thy robes;

So long, sure-found beneath the sylvan shed,
Shall Fancy, Friendship, Science, rose-lipp'd Health,   50
   Thy gentlest influence own,
    And hymn thy fav'rite name!

ODE TO PEACE.

O THOU who bad'st thy turtles bear
Swift from his grasp thy golden hair,
   And sought'st thy native skies:
When War, by vultures drawn from far,
To Britain bent his iron car,   5
   And bad his storm arise!

Tir'd of his rude tyrannic sway,
Our youth shall fix some festive day,
   His sullen shrines to burn:

49–52. So long, regardful of thy quiet rule,
    Shall Fancy, Friendship, Science, smiling Peace,
      Thy gentlest influence own,
       And love thy fav'rite name!   — 1747.
   49. So long, sure-found beneath thy sylvan shed,   — 1753.

But thou who hear'st the turning spheres,   10
What sounds may charm thy partial ears,
   And gain thy blest return !

O Peace, thy injur'd robes up-bind !
O rise, and leave not one behind
   Of all thy beamy train !   15
The British lion, goddess sweet,
Lies stretch'd on earth to kiss thy feet,
   And own thy holier reign.

Let others court thy transient smile,
But come to grace thy western isle,   20
   By warlike Honour led !
And, while around her ports rejoice,
While all her sons adore thy choice,
   With him for ever wed !

THE MANNERS. AN ODE.

FAREWELL, for clearer ken design'd,
The dim-discover'd tracts of Mind:
Truths which, from Action's paths retir'd,
My silent search in vain requir'd !
No more my sail that deep explores,   5
No more I search those magic shores,
What regions part the world of Soul,
Or whence thy streams, Opinion, roll :
If e'er I round such fairy field,
Some pow'r impart the spear and shield   10
At which the wizard Passions fly,
By which the giant Follies die !
   Farewell the Porch, whose roof is seen
Arch'd with th' enliv'ning olive's green :

Where Science, prank'd in tissu'd vest,　　15
By Reason, Pride, and Fancy drest,
Comes like a bride so trim array'd,
To wed with Doubt in Plato's shade!
　　Youth of the quick uncheated sight,
Thy walks, Observance, more invite!　　20
O thou who lov'st that ampler range
Where Life's wide prospects round thee change,
And, with her mingling sons ally'd,
Throw'st the prattling page aside,
To me in converse sweet impart　　25
To read in man the native heart,
To learn, where Science sure is found,
From Nature as she lives around,
And, gazing oft her mirror true,
By turns each shifting image view!　　30
Till meddling Art's officious lore
Reverse the lessons taught before,
Alluring from a safer rule
To dream in her enchanted school,
Thou, Heav'n, whate'er of great we boast,　　35
Hast blest this social Science most.
　　Retiring hence to thoughtful cell,
As Fancy breathes her potent spell,
Not vain she finds the charmful task:
In pageant quaint, in motley mask,　　40
Behold, before her musing eyes,
The countless Manners round her rise;
While, ever varying as they pass,
To some Contempt applies her glass:
With these the white-rob'd maids combine　　45
And those the laughing satyrs join!
But who is he whom now she views,
In robe of wild contending hues?

Thou by the Passions nurs'd, I greet
The comic sock that binds thy feet !   50
O Humour, thou whose name is known
To Britain's favor'd isle alone,
Me too amidst thy band admit,
There where the young-ey'd healthful Wit
(Whose jewels in his crisped hair   55
Are plac'd each other's beams to share,
Whom no delights from thee divide)
In laughter loos'd attends thy side !
    By old Miletus,[1] who so long
Has ceas'd his love-inwoven song :   60
By all you taught the Tuscan maids,
In chang'd Italia's modern shades :
By him [2] whose knight's distinguish'd name
Refin'd a nation's lust of fame ;
Whose tales ev'n now, with echoes sweet,   65
Castilia's Moorish hills repeat :
Or him [3] whom Seine's blue nymphs deplore,
In watchet weeds, on Gallia's shore,
Who drew the sad Sicilian maid,
By virtues in her sire betray'd :   70
O Nature boon, from whom proceed
Each forceful thought, each prompted deed,
If but from thee I hope to feel,
On all my heart imprint thy seal!
Let some retreating cynic find   75
Those oft-turn'd scrolls I leave behind :
The Sports and I this hour agree
To rove thy scene-full world with thee !

---

[1] Alluding to the *Milesian Tales*, some of the earliest romances.—C.
[2] Cervantes.— C.
[3] Monsieur Le Sage, author of the incomparable *Adventures of Gil Blas de Santillane*, who died in Paris in the year 1745. — C.

THE PASSIONS.

AN ODE FOR MUSIC.

WHEN Music, heav'nly maid, was young,
While yet in early Greece she sung,
The Passions oft, to hear her shell,
Throng'd around her magic cell,
Exulting, trembling, raging, fainting,   5
Possest beyond the Muse's painting ;
By turns they felt the glowing mind
Disturb'd, delighted, rais'd, refin'd :
Till once, 't is said, when all were fir'd,
Fill'd with fury, rapt, inspir'd,   10
From the supporting myrtles round
They snatch'd her instruments of sound ;
And as they oft had heard apart
Sweet lessons of her forceful art,
Each, for madness rul'd the hour,   15
Would prove his own expressive pow'r.

First Fear his hand, its skill to try,
    Amid the chords bewilder'd laid,
And back recoil'd, he knew not why,
    Ev'n at the sound himself had made.   20

Next Anger rush'd ; his eyes, on fire,
    In lightnings own'd his secret stings ;
In one rude clash he struck the lyre,
    And swept with hurried hand the strings.

With woful measures wan Despair   25
    Low sullen sounds his grief beguil'd ;
A solemn, strange, and mingled air ;
    'T was sad by fits, by starts 't was wild.

But thou, O Hope, with eyes so fair,
  What was thy delightful measure? 30
Still it whisper'd promis'd pleasure,
  And bad the lovely scenes at distance hail !
Still would her touch the strain prolong,
  And from the rocks, the woods, the vale,
She call'd on Echo still thro' all the song ; 35
  And where her sweetest theme she chose,
  A soft responsive voice was heard at ev'ry close,
And Hope enchanted smil'd, and wav'd her golden
    hair.

And longer had she sung, — but with a frown
    Revenge impatient rose ; 40
He threw his blood-stain'd sword in thunder down
    And with a with'ring look
  The war-denouncing trumpet took,
And blew a blast so loud and dread,
Were ne'er prophetic sounds so full of woe. 45
    And ever and anon he beat
    The doubling drum with furious heat ;
  And tho' sometimes, each dreary pause between,
    Dejected Pity, at his side,
    Her soul-subduing voice apply'd, 50
Yet still he kept his wild unalter'd mien,
While each strain'd ball of sight seem'd bursting
    from his head.

Thy numbers, Jealousy, to nought were fix'd,
  Sad proof of thy distressful state ;
Of diff'ring themes the veering song was mix'd, 55
  And now it courted Love, now raving call'd on
    Hate.

With eyes uprais'd, as one inspir'd,
Pale Melancholy sate retir'd,

And from her wild sequester'd seat,
In notes by distance made more sweet, 60
Pour'd thro' the mellow horn her pensive soul :
 And, dashing soft from rocks around,
 Bubbling runnels join'd the sound ;
Thro' glades and glooms the mingled measure
  stole ;
 Or o'er some haunted stream with fond delay 65
  Round an holy calm diffusing,
  Love of peace and lonely musing,
 In hollow murmurs died away.

But O how alter'd was its sprightlier tone,
When Chearfulness, a nymph of healthiest hue, 70
 Her bow across her shoulder flung,
 Her buskins gemm'd with morning dew,
Blew an inspiring air, that dale and thicket rung,
 The hunter's call to faun and dryad known !
 The oak-crown'd sisters, and their chaste-ey'd
  queen, 75
 Satyrs, and sylvan boys, were seen,
 Peeping from forth their alleys green ;
Brown Exercise rejoic'd to hear,
 And Sport leapt up, and seiz'd his beechen spear.

Last came Joy's ecstatic trial. 80
He, with viny crown advancing,
 First to the lively pipe his hand addrest ;
But soon he saw the brisk awak'ning viol,
 Whose sweet entrancing voice he lov'd the best.
  They would have thought, who heard the strain, 85
  They saw in Tempe's vale her native maids,
  Amidst the festal sounding shades,
To some unwearied minstrel dancing,
 While, as his flying fingers kiss'd the strings,

Love fram'd with Mirth a gay fantastic round ;   90
Loose were her tresses seen, her zone unbound,
And he, amidst his frolic play,
As if he would the charming air repay,
Shook thousand odours from his dewy wings.

O Music, sphere-descended maid,   95
Friend of Pleasure, Wisdom's aid,
Why, goddess, why, to us deny'd,
Lay'st thou thy antient lyre aside?
As in that lov'd Athenian bow'r
You learn'd an all-commanding pow'r,   100
Thy mimic soul, O nymph endear'd,
Can well recall what then it heard.
Where is thy native simple heart,
Devote to Virtue, Fancy, Art?
Arise as in that elder time,   105
Warm, energic, chaste, sublime !
Thy wonders, in that godlike age,
Fill thy recording sister's page —
'T is said, and I believe the tale,
Thy humblest reed could more prevail,   110
Had more of strength, diviner rage,
Than all which charms this laggard age,
Ev'n all at once together found,
Cæcilia's mingled world of sound.
O bid our vain endeavours cease,   115
Revive the just designs of Greece,
Return in all thy simple state,
Confirm the tales her sons relate !

LATER ODES.

ODE ON THE DEATH OF MR. THOMSON.

The scene of the following stanzas is suppos'd to lie on the Thames,
near Richmond.

In yonder grave a druid lies,
　　Where slowly winds the stealing wave.
The year's best sweets shall duteous rise
　　To deck its poet's sylvan grave.

In yon deep bed of whisp'ring reeds　　　　　5
　　His airy harp [1] shall now be laid,
That he whose heart in sorrow bleeds
　　May love thro' life the soothing shade.

Then maids and youths shall linger here ;
　　And while its sounds at distance swell,　　10
Shall sadly seem in Pity's ear
　　To hear the Woodland Pilgrim's knell.

Remembrance oft shall haunt the shore
　　When Thames in summer wreaths is drest,
And oft suspend the dashing oar　　　　　15
　　To bid his gentle spirit rest.

And oft as Ease and Health retire
　　To breezy lawn, or forest deep,
The friend shall view yon whit'ning spire,[2]
　　And mid the varied landscape weep.　　　20

---

[1] The harp of Æolus, of which see a description in *The Castle of
ndolence.* — C.

[2] Richmond church. — C.

But thou who own'st that earthy bed,
  Ah, what will ev'ry dirge avail,
Or tears which Love and Pity shed,
  That mourn beneath the gliding sail?

Yet lives there one whose heedless eye   25
  Shall scorn thy pale shrine glimm'ring near?
With him, sweet bard, may Fancy die,
  And Joy desert the blooming year!

But thou, lorn stream, whose sullen tide
  No sedge-crown'd sisters now attend,   30
Now waft me from the green hill's side
  Whose cold turf hides the buried friend.

And see, the fairy valleys fade;
  Dun night has veil'd the solemn view.
Yet once again, dear parted shade,   35
  Meek Nature's child, again adieu!

The genial meads, assign'd to bless
  Thy life, shall mourn thy early doom;
Their hinds and shepherd girls shall dress
  With simple hands thy rural tomb.   40

Long, long, thy stone and pointed clay
  Shall melt the musing Briton's eyes;
O vales and wild woods, shall he say,
  In yonder grave your druid lies!

AN ODE ON THE POPULAR SUPERSTITIONS OF THE HIGHLANDS OF SCOTLAND,

CONSIDERED AS THE SUBJECT OF POETRY.

I.

H——, thou return'st from Thames, whose naiads long
   Have seen thee ling'ring, with a fond delay,
   'Mid those soft friends, whose hearts, some future day,
Shall melt, perhaps, to hear thy tragic song.
Go, not unmindful of that cordial youth   5
   Whom, long-endear'd, thou leav'st by Lavant's side;
Together let us wish him lasting truth,
   And joy untainted, with his destined bride.
Go! nor regardless, while these numbers boast
   My short-liv'd bliss, forget my social name;   10
But think far off how, on the Southern coast,
   I met thy friendship with an equal flame!
Fresh to that soil thou turn'st, whose ev'ry vale
   Shall prompt the poet, and his song demand:
To thee thy copious subjects ne'er shall fail;   15
   Thou need'st but take the pencil to thy hand,
And paint what all believe who own thy genial land.

II.

There must thou wake perforce thy Doric quill;
   'T is Fancy's land to which thou sett'st thy feet,
   Where still, 't is said, the fairy people meet   20
Beneath each birken shade on mead or hill.

---

1. Home, thou return'st from Thames, whose naiads long
                             — Anon. ed.
3. Fresh to that soil thou turn'st, where ev'ry vale   — Anon. ed.
6. Thou need'st but take thy pencil to thy hand,   — Anon. ed.

There each trim lass that skims the milky store
  To the swart tribes their creamy bowl allots ;
By night they sip it round the cottage door,
  While airy minstrels warble jocund notes.   25
There ev'ry herd, by sad experience, knows
  How, wing'd with fate, their elf-shot arrows fly ;
When the sick ewe her summer food foregoes,
  Or, stretch'd on earth, the heart-smit heifers lie.
Such airy beings awe th' untutor'd swain :   30
  Nor thou, thou learn'd, his homelier thoughts neglect ;
Let thy sweet Muse the rural faith sustain :
  These are the themes of simple, sure effect,
That add new conquests to her boundless reign,
And fill, with double force, her heart-commanding strain. 35

III.

Ev'n yet preserv'd, how often may'st thou hear,
  Where to the pole the boreal mountains run,
  Taught by the father to his list'ning son,
Strange lays, whose pow'r had charm'd a Spenser's ear.
At ev'ry pause, before thy mind possest,   4
  Old Runic bards shall seem to rise around,
With uncouth lyres, in many-colour'd vest,
  Their matted hair with boughs fantastic crown'd :
Whether thou bid'st the well-taught hind repeat
  The choral dirge that mourns some chieftain brave, 4
When ev'ry shrieking maid her bosom beat,
  And strew'd with choicest herbs his scented grave ;
Or whether, sitting in the shepherd's shiel,
  Thou hear'st some sounding tale of war's alarms,
When, at the bugle's call, with fire and steel,   5

---

23. To the swart tribes their creamy bowls allots ;   — Anon. ed.
44. Whether thou bid'st the well-taught hind relate   — MS.

The sturdy clans pour'd forth their bony swarms,
And hostile brothers met to prove each other's arms.

IV.

'T is thine to sing, how, framing hideous spells,
  In Sky's lone isle the gifted wizard seer,
  Lodg'd in the wintry cave with [   ]   55
Or in the depth of Uist's dark forests dwells :
How they whose sight such dreary dreams engross,
  With their own visions oft astonish'd droop,
When o'er the wat'ry strath or quaggy moss
  They see the gliding ghosts unbodied troop ;   60
Or if in sports, or on the festive green,
  Their [   ] glance some fated youth descry,
Who, now perhaps in lusty vigour seen
  And rosy health, shall soon lamented die.
For them the viewless forms of air obey,   65
  Their bidding heed, and at their beck repair.
They know what spirit brews the stormful day,
  And, heartless, oft like moody madness stare
To see the phantom train their secret work prepare.

V.

[This stanza, comprising lines 70–86, was missing in
the manuscript.]

51. The sturdy clans pour'd forth their brawny swarms,
                                     — Anon. ed.
55, 56.   Lodg'd in the wintry cave with Fate's fell spear ;
      Or in the depth of Uist's dark forest dwells : — Anon. ed.
56. Or in the gloom of Uist's dark forests dwells :   — MS.
58. With their own visions oft afflicted droop,   — MS.
62. Their destin'd glance some fated youth descry, — Anon. ed.
66. Their bidding mark, and at their beck repair.   — MS.
70–86. To monarchs dear, some hundred miles astray,
      Oft have they seen Fate give the fatal blow !
      The seer, in Sky, shriek'd as the blood did flow,
  When headless Charles warm on the scaffold lay !

VI.

[The first eight lines of this stanza, lines 87–94 of the
poem, were missing in the manuscript.]

What tho' far off, from some dark dell espied,   95
 His glimm'ring mazes cheer th' excursive sight,
Yet turn, ye wand'rers, turn your steps aside,
 Nor trust the guidance of that faithless light;
For, watchful, lurking 'mid th' unrustling reed,
 At those mirk hours the wily monster lies,   100
And listens oft to hear the passing steed,
 And frequent round him rolls his sullen eyes,
If chance his savage wrath may some weak wretch surprise.

  As Boreas threw his young Aurora forth,
   In the first year of the first George's reign,
  And battles rag'd in welkin of the North,
   They mourn'd in air, fell, fell Rebellion slain !
  And as, of late, they joy'd in Preston's fight,
   Saw at sad Falkirk all their hopes near crown'd,
  They rav'd, divining, thro' their second sight,
   Pale, red Culloden, where these hopes were drown'd !
  Illustrious William ! Britain's guardian name !
   One William sav'd us from a tyrant's stroke ;
  He, for a sceptre, gain'd heroic fame ;
   But thou, more glorious, Slavery's chain hast broke,
  To reign a private man, and bow to Freedom's yoke !
            — Anon. ed.

87-94. These, too, thou 'lt sing ! for well thy magic Muse
   Can to the topmost heav'n of grandeur soar !
   Or stoop to wail the swain that is no more !
   Ah, homely swains ! your homeward steps ne'er lose ;
   Let not dank Will mislead you to the heath :
    Dancing in mirky night, o'er fen and lake,
   He glows, to draw you downward to your death,
    In his bewitch'd, low, marshy willow brake ! — Anon. ed.
 100. At those sad hours the wily monster lies,   — MS.

VII.

Ah, luckless swain, o'er all unblest indeed !
 Whom, late bewilder'd in the dank, dark fen,   105
  Far from his flocks and smoking hamlet then,
To that sad spot [   ]
On him, enrag'd, the fiend, in angry mood,
 Shall never look with Pity's kind concern,
But instant, furious, raise the whelming flood   110
  O'er its drown'd bank, forbidding all return.
Or, if he meditate his wish'd escape
 To some dim hill that seems uprising near,
To his faint eye the grim and grisly shape,
  In all its terrors clad, shall wild appear.   115
Meantime, the wat'ry surge shall round him rise,
 Pour'd sudden forth from ev'ry swelling source.
What now remains but tears and hopeless sighs?
 His fear-shook limbs have lost their youthly force,
And down the waves he floats, a pale and breathless
  corse.   120

VIII.

For him, in vain, his anxious wife shall wait,
 Or wander forth to meet him on his way;
  For him, in vain, at to-fall of the day,
His babes shall linger at th' unclosing gate.
Ah, ne'er shall he return ! Alone, if night   125
 Her travell'd limbs in broken slumbers steep,
With dropping willows drest, his mournful sprite
  Shall visit sad, perchance, her silent sleep :

107. To that sad spot where hums the sedgy weed : — Anon. ed.
111. O'er its drown'd banks, forbidding all return. — Anon. ed.
124. His babes shall linger at the cottage gate.   — MS.
127. With drooping willows drest, his mournful sprite — Anon. ed.

Then he, perhaps, with moist and wat'ry hand,
    Shall fondly seem to press her shudd'ring cheek,   130
And with his blue-swoln face before her stand,
    And, shiv'ring cold, these piteous accents speak :
" Pursue, dear wife, thy daily toils pursue
    At dawn or dusk, industrious as before ;
Nor e'er of me one hapless thought renew,   135
    While I lie welt'ring on the ozier'd shore,
Drown'd by the kælpie's wrath, nor e'er shall aid thee
      more ! "

IX.

Unbounded is thy range ; with varied stile
    Thy Muse may, like those feath'ry tribes which spring
    From their rude rocks, extend her skirting wing   140
Round the moist marge of each cold Hebrid isle,
To that hoar pile which still its ruin shows :
    In whose small vaults a pigmy-folk is found,
Whose bones the delver with his spade upthrows,
    And culls them, wond'ring, from the hallow'd ground ! 145
Or thither, where, beneath the show'ry West,
    The mighty kings of three fair realms are laid :
Once foes, perhaps, together now they rest ;
    No slaves revere them, and no wars invade :
Yet frequent now, at midnight's solemn hour,   150
    The rifted mounds their yawning cells unfold,
And forth the monarchs stalk with sov'reign pow'r,
    In pageant robes, and wreath'd with sheeny gold,
And on their twilight tombs aerial council hold.

130. Shall seem to press her cold and shudd'ring cheek,   — MS.
133. " Proceed, dear wife, thy daily toils pursue "   — MS.
135. Nor e'er of me one helpless thought renew,   — Anon. ed.
138. Unbounded is thy range ; with varied skill   — Anon. ed.
150. Yet frequent now at midnight solemn hour,   — Anon. ed.

X.

But O, o'er all, forget not Kilda's race,   155
   On whose bleak rocks, which brave the wasting tides,
   Fair Nature's daughter, Virtue, yet abides.
Go, just as they, their blameless manners trace !
Then to my ear transmit some gentle song
   Of those whose lives are yet sincere and plain,   160
Their bounded walks the rugged cliffs along,
   And all their prospect but the wintry main.
With sparing temp'rance, at the needful time,
   They drain the sainted spring, or, hunger-prest,
Along th' Atlantic rock undreading climb,   165
   And of its eggs despoil the solan's nest.
Thus blest in primal innocence they live,
   Suffic'd and happy with that frugal fare
Which tasteful toil and hourly danger give.
   Hard is their shallow soil, and bleak and bare ;   170
Nor ever vernal bee was heard to murmur there !

XI.

Nor need'st thou blush, that such false themes engage
   Thy gentle mind, of fairer stores possest ;
   For not alone they touch the village breast,
But fill'd in elder time th' historic page.   175
There Shakespear's self, with ev'ry garland crown'd,
   [   ]
n musing hour, his wayward Sisters found,
   And with their terrors drest the magic scene.
   From them he sung when, 'mid his bold design,   180

164. They drain the scented spring, or, hunger-prest,
                                    — Anon. ed.
177, 178. Flew to those fairy climes his fancy sheen,
       In musing hour ; his wayward Sisters found,   — Anon. ed.

Before the Scot afflicted and aghast,
  The shadowy kings of Banquo's fated line
    Thro' the dark cave in gleamy pageant past.
Proceed, nor quit the tales which, simply told,
  Could once so well my answ'ring bosom pierce ;   185
Proceed ! in forceful sounds and colours bold,
  The native legends of thy land rehearse ;
To such adapt thy lyre and suit thy pow'rful verse.

XII.

In scenes like these, which, daring to depart
  From sober truth, are still to nature true,   190
    And call forth fresh delight to Fancy's view,
Th' heroic muse employ'd her Tasso's art !
How have I trembled, when, at Tancred's stroke,
  Its gushing blood the gaping cypress pour'd ;
When each live plant with mortal accents spoke,   195
  And the wild blast upheav'd the vanish'd sword !
How have I sat, when pip'd the pensive wind,
  To hear his harp, by British Fairfax strung.
Prevailing poet, whose undoubting mind
  Believ'd the magic wonders which he sung !   200
Hence at each sound imagination glows;
    [   ]
Hence his warm lay with softest sweetness flows;

---

186. Proceed ! in forceful sounds and colour bold,   — Anon. ed.
193–196. How have I trembled, when, at Tancred's side,
        Like him I stalk'd, and all his passions felt;
        When, charm'd by Ismen, thro' the forest wide,
        Bark'd in each plant, a talking spirit dwelt!   — MS.
201–205. Hence, sure to charm, his early numbers flow,
        Tho' faithful, sweet; tho' strong, of simple kind.
      Hence, with each theme, he bids the bosom glow,
        While his warm lays an easy passage find,
      Pour'd thro' each inmost nerve, and lull th' harmonious
        ear.   — MS.

Melting it flows, pure, num'rous, strong, and clear,
And fills th' impassion'd heart, and wins th' harmoni-
     ous ear.   205

XIII.

All hail, ye scenes that o'er my soul prevail,
    Ye [   ] friths and lakes which, far away,
    Are by smooth Annan fill'd, or past'ral Tay,
Or Don's romantic springs ; at distance, hail !
The time shall come when I, perhaps, may tread   210
    Your lowly glens, o'erhung with spreading broom,
Or o'er your stretching heaths by fancy led :
    [   ]
Then will I dress once more the faded bow'r,
    Where Jonson sat in Drummond's [   ] shade,   215
Or crop from Tiviot's dale each [   ]
    And mourn on Yarrow's banks [   ]
Meantime, ye Pow'rs that on the plains which bore
    The cordial youth, on Lothian's plains, attend,
Where'er he dwell, on hill or lowly muir,   220
    To him I lose your kind protection lend,
And, touch'd with love like mine, preserve my absent
    friend !

202. Tho' strong, yet sweet——   — MS.
202. Hence, at each picture, vivid life starts here ! — Anon. ed.
204. Melting it flows, pure, murm'ring, strong, and clear,
                                     — Anon. ed.
207. Ye splendid friths and lakes which, far away,
                                     — Anon. ed.
213. Or o'er your mountains creep, in awful gloom !
                                     — Anon. ed.
215–217.   Where Jonson sat in Drummond's classic shade ;
        Or crop from Tiviotdale each lyric flow'r,
        And mourn, on Yarrow's banks, where Willy 's laid !
                                   —Anon. ed.
220. Where'er Home dwells, on hill or lowly moor,   — Anon. ed.

N O T E S.

N O T E S.[1]

TO MISS AURELIA C———R. (3)

This is probably Collins's earliest printed poem.[2] It appeared in *The Gentleman's Magazine* for January, 1739, over the signature "Amasius." That Collins was the author is affirmed in a sketch of his life in Fawkes and Woty's *Poetical Calendar*, December, 1763, and in Johnson's *Life of Collins*. Other poems by "Amasius" appeared in *The Gentleman's Magazine* in 1739, 1740, 1741, and 1743; but they are so poor that Collins can hardly have written them, as a sample will show :

> Assisted by the telescope,
> Yon mighty orbs survey,
> How regular they whirl around
> The planetary way!

SONNET. (3)

These lines, after the fashion of the day loosely styled a sonnet, were published in *The Gentleman's Magazine* for October, 1739, and signed "Delicatulus." They are attributed to Collins by Joseph Warton. "In a magazine [*The Gentleman's Magazine*, where the three poems mentioned are printed together] I find the following memorandum, in Dr. Warton's hand-writing : — ' P. 545. *Sappho's Advice* was written by me, then at Winchester school ; the next by Tomkyns ; and the sonnet by Collins.   J. Warton.' " — John Wooll, in his *Memoirs of Warton*, London, 1806, p. 107. The poem was noticed in the next issue of the magazine in a letter to the editor which Wooll says was written by Johnson (although Chalmers, in his sketch of Warton's life in his *English Poets*, says Wooll was mistaken) : " The least, which is a

---

1 The figures in parenthesis after the titles of the poems, and the figures in brackets at the tops of the pages, refer to pages of the text.

2 For reference to an earlier poem, perhaps by him, see *Introduction*, p. xiii.

favorite of mine, carries a force mixed with tenderness, and an uncommon elevation." A good deal of allowance must be made for the fact that this letter was written, as its last paragraph shows, to puff the magazine; but the praise of Collins's poem, although too serious for such a trifle (coming from Johnson it reminds one of an elephant toying with a comfit), seems less perfunctory than the rest of the letter and may have helped to draw the two men together a few years later.

1. **wanton** = *playful;* perhaps *coquettish* here.

SONG. (3)

The authenticity of this poem is doubtful. It was printed anonymously in *The Public Advertiser*, London, March 7, 1788, where the present editor stumbled upon it recently; whether it had appeared earlier is uncertain. It was printed among Collins's poems in Johnson's *English Poets*, 1790, in Anderson's *Poets of Great Britain*, 1794, and in Chalmers's *English Poets*, 1810. It was not contained in Park's *British Poets*, 1805, but apparently was added in a later edition. "Mr. Park (who inserted it on an additional leaf) observes to me that he has now forgotten on what authority he gave it as the production of Collins, but that he must have been satisfied of its genuineness at the time he reprinted it, else he would not have done so." — Dyce, in his edition of Collins, London and Oxford, 1827, p. 208. The Aldine *Collins* (London, 1894, p. 101) has the following note : "A manuscript copy in the collection recently belonging to Mr. Upcott, and now in the British Museum, is headed, ' Written by Collins when at Winchester School. From a Manuscript.'" A recent search at the British Museum by the present editor failed to discover any trace of such a manuscript.

A comparison with the following lines from Ophelia's song (*Hamlet*, iv, 5) will show how far "the sentiments" are "borrowed from Shakespear" :

> He is dead and gone, lady,
> 　He is dead and gone;
> At his head a grass-green turf,
> 　At his heels a stone.

> White his shroud as the mountain snow,
> 　Larded with sweet flowers;
> Which bewept to the grave did go
> 　With true-love showers.

> They bore him barefaced on the bier;
> And in his grave rain'd many a tear.
>
> And will he not come again?
> And will he not come again?
>   No, no, he is dead:
>   Go to thy death-bed:
> He never will come again.

2. lowland seems to have been the earlier reading (*The Public Advertiser*, 1788; Anderson's *Poets of Great Britain*, 1794); certainly it is the better: the lowliness of the hamlets is not relevant, while the fact that they are "lowland," in the "vale" where Damon was known and loved, is relevant.

18. who lov'd is less obvious than *belov'd* (for which there seems to be no authority except that cited in the footnote), and it adds an active element to the character of Damon, who would otherwise be wholly passive, a mere target for affection.

VERSES WRITTEN ON A PAPER, ETC. (4)

On what evidence this poem was ascribed to Collins does not appear. It is clearly in his manner. It was published, apparently for the first time, along with several other of Collins's poems in Pearch's *Collection of Poems* (London, 3d ed., 1775, vol. II). In the present edition it is placed among the early poems wholly on internal evidence. It seems to belong to the days of the poet's younger and mildly amorous muse; but it shows more maturity of manner than the first two poems, and may have been written, in an idle hour, as late as the earlier odes.

6. shepherd's, *i.e.*, the poet's.

haunted, *i.e.*, by "flattering dreams"; see l. 22.

19. Cf. *Paradise Lost*, iv, 310, 311:

> With coy submission, modest pride,
> And sweet, reluctant, amorous delay.

22, 24. his refers to *shepherd's*, l. 6.

A SONG FROM SHAKESPEAR'S CYMBELINE. (6)

This song was published in 1744, in the same folio with the *Epistle to Sir Thomas Hanmer;* see p. lxxx. In October, 1749, it was reprinted, with changes, in *The Gentleman's Magazine.* In Nichols's *Literary Anecdotes* (London, 1812, vol. V, p. 53), is preserved the following reminiscence by Sir John Hawkins:

"I remember that, calling in on him [Cave, proprietor of *The Gentleman's Magazine*] once, he gave me to read the beautiful poem of Collins, written for Shakspeare's *Cymbeline,* 'To fair Fidele's grassy tomb,' which, though adapted to a particular circumstance in the play, Cave was for inserting in his magazine without any reference to the subject. I told him it would lose of its beauty if it were so published: this he could not see; nor could he be convinced of the propriety of the name *Fidele:* he thought *Pastora* a better, and so printed it."

The other changes, also, were doubtless unauthorized; and, as a bit of literary history illustrating the prevailing carelessness and lack of conscience in such matters then, it is worth while to give the entire list: Title, *Elegiac Song;* 1. *Pastora's;* 7. *swains* for *lads;* 11. *But* for *The* (repeating the sentence-structure of the preceding stanza); 12. *bed* for *grave;* 17. *chiding* for *howling;* 18. *tempest* for *tempests;* 19. *flocks* for *chace* (still further obliterating the poem's relation to *Cymbeline:* Guiderius and Arviragus were hunters, not shepherds); 21. *lovely* for *lonely;* 23. *can* for *could* (Collins's thought was, 'Beloved to extreme old age, when life *could* have charmed no more even if it had been continued').

The misspelling of "Guiderius" may have been a printer's error, but very likely it was one of Collins's careless slips.

The atmosphere of tender grace pervading the poem is peculiarly Collins's own; but a comparison with *Cymbeline,* iv, 2, shows that the inspiration of the lines was a fine sympathy with the spirit of Shakspere's scene as a whole, although the likeness between the two songs is slight. Dyce compares l. 5 with *Cymbeline,* iv, 2, 278: Ghost unlaid forbear thee; l. 9 with 277: Nor no witchcraft charm thee; l. 11 with 217: With female fairies will his tomb be haunted; stanza 4 with 224–229:

> the ruddock would,
> With charitable bill, — O bill, sore-shaming
> Those rich-left heirs that let their fathers lie
> Without a monument! — bring thee all this;
> Yea, and furr'd moss besides, when flowers are none,
> To winter-ground thy corse.

Compare also, for their spirit of delicate love, lines 218–224 with the poem as a whole :

> With fairest flowers
> While summer lasts and I live here, Fidele,
> I'll sweeten thy sad grave: thou shalt not lack
> The flower that's like thy face, pale primrose, nor
> The azured harebell, like thy veins, no, nor
> The leaf of eglantine, whom not to slander,
> Out-sweeten'd not thy breath.

4. breathing spring. Dyce compares Pope's *Messiah*, 24 :

> With all the incense of the breathing spring.

ORIENTAL ECLOGUES. (7)

The *Eclogues* were first published in January, 1742 (see *The Gentleman's Magazine*, January, 1742, register of books), with the title, *Persian Eclogues* (see p. lxxix). Five hundred copies were printed : " Mr. Andrew Millar, Dr. Dec. 10, 1741. *Persian Eclogues*, 1½ shts., No. 500. Reprinting ½ sht." — Ledger of Woodfall, the printer, from *Notes and Queries*, 1st series, vol. XI, p. 419. In January, 1757 (see *The Gentleman's Magazine*, January, 1757, register of books), a second edition, considerably revised, with the title of *Oriental Eclogues*, appeared (see p. lxxxi).

" Mr. Collins wrote his eclogues when he was about seventeen years old, at Winchester school, and, as I well remember, had just been reading that volume of Salmon's *Modern History* which described Persia ; which determined him to lay the scene of these pieces [there], as being productive of new images and sentiments. In his maturer years he was accustomed to speak very contemptuously of them, calling them his Irish Eclogues, and saying they had not in them one spark of Orientalism ; and desiring me to erase a motto he had prefixed to them in a copy he gave me ; — quos primus equis oriens afflavit anhelis. VIRG. He was greatly mortified that they found more readers and admirers than his odes." — Joseph Warton, in his edition of Pope, London, 1797, vol. I, p. 61.

The statement about the motto is inconsistent with what Warton wrote in the copy given to him by Collins (see p. lxxix) ; either Warton's memory was at fault, or Collins gave him another copy in early years.

The motto is not the entire line (*Georgics*, i, 250), *nosque* being omitted before *ubi*. Collins originally wrote *quos* instead of *nosque ubi;* this may perhaps indicate that he had forgotten the context and took the line as a designation of the Orientals, those on whom the sun shines first in its progress westward; but it is more likely that he meant to ignore the context and let the words be taken to mean what they appear to mean when standing alone.

In the 1742 edition the following lines from Cicero's *Oration for the Poet Archias* preceded the *Preface:* Quod si non hic tantus fructus ostenderetur, et si ex his studiis delectatio sola peteretur; tamen, ut opinor, hanc animi remissionem humanissimam ac liberalissimam judicaretis.

The following passage from Salmon's *Modern History* evidently suggested to Collins much of what is said or implied in the *Preface* and *Eclogue the First* about Persian poets and poetry:

"Every great man has a poet in his family, and no entertainment is complete unless a poet be there to oblige the company with his compositions. There are many of them who frequent the coffee houses, and publick places of resort, where they repeat their poems to the audience. . . . The King himself entertains several as his domesticks. . . . The subject of their poems is generally some piece of morality, or philosophy. . . . One method which the antients took to preserve the memory of their great actions, was to make them the subject of their songs, and sing them in their assemblies, and at their festivals, as is the custom in Persia at this day. . . . The thoughts are noble and elevated, their expressions soft; . . . their allusions are delicate, and abundance of hyperbole you must expect in all their figures. Love is sometimes the subject of their poems, as well as morality and history; but nothing immodest . . . is ever the subject of their verse." — *Modern History: or, the Present State of All Nations,* by Thomas Salmon, London, 1744, 3d ed., vol. I, p. 337.

For the reference in the *Preface* to Hosseyn, see pp. 89, 90.

———

ECLOGUE THE FIRST. (11)

The selection of morning as the time for giving all this good advice to "the fair and young" is arbitrary, unless there be an allusion to the threadbare figure of youth as the morning of life.

6. This sentiment must have met with the approval of Johnson; it is akin to the theme of his *Rasselas.*

12. The line contravenes a poetic commonplace of the age, according to which rural life was credited with superior virtues as well as superior happiness. Cf. Gray's *Elegy,* Goldsmith's *Deserted Village,* and Collins's own *Ode on the Popular Superstitions of the Highlands of Scotland*, stanza 10.

13. The readings of the text of 1742 show what difficulty Collins had in keeping himself in Persia ; he came back to Europe in *Eastern* and *od'rous*. Cf. l. 69, the earlier reading.

17. Tigris'. Bagdat, on the Tigris, long a bone of contention between Persia and Turkey, was retaken by Abbas the Great before the time when the *Eclogues* are supposed to have been written ; the reference is therefore in keeping with the fiction. Cf. *maids of Bagdat*, l. 70.

19. The correction of *ye* to *you*, here and in ll. 21, 25, 49, is made in Collins's handwriting in the copy of the *Persian Eclogues* given by him to J. Warton.

23–25. The thought is obscure and awkwardly expressed. Apparently the meaning is that the Persian maids have eyes like the morning and flower-like beauty, which inspire love.

23. loves supplies. An instance of what Johnson meant, in his censure of Collins's verse, by lines " clogged and impeded with clusters of consonants."

32. A comparison with the earlier reading is rather amusing ; the poet's opinion of pearls seems to have changed in the interval.

33–36. The balanced sentence-structure and the antithesis show the influence of the prevailing fashion in verse upon Collins's early manner.

37, 38. A couplet much in the neat style of Pope.

46. Immortal Truth. The improvement upon the earlier reading is manifest. Truth is here male, and therefore *fair-ey'd* is scarcely appropriate ; certainly it is weaker than *immortal*.

47. fair maids! ye Virtues. The daughters of Truth and Wisdom. **come away!** *i.e.*, to Persia, and bring the Golden Age again.

51–68. The conception of a train of personified virtues accompanying Modesty is manifestly borrowed from *L'Allegro* and *Il Penseroso*, where Mirth and Melancholy are similarly attended.

53. An awkward inversion for the sake of a rhyme.

53, 54. In the text of 1742 these lines greatly needed revision. The first line had only two significant words, *come* and *Modesty ; O* and *thou* were there expletives, and *as they decree* merely repeated *so the Fates ordain* of l. 51. The second line contained an unnatural and stale conceit, and diverted attention from the maids of Bagdat to the effect of the coming Golden Age upon the complexion of roses.

57–62. The description of Chastity is not a success. We do not like this Chastity ; she is too suspicious and self-conscious by half.

59, 60. "In some parts of the East, antelopes are taken by hawks, trained purposely to take them." — *Critical Essays*, by John Scott, London, 1785, p. 163.

64. Faith, *i.e.*, Fidelity.

65. desponding seems too strong a word; the idea, apparently, is the negative one of freedom from over-confidence.

down-cast eyes. Cf. *Il Penseroso*, 43:

> With a sad leaden downward cast.

70. One very much doubts whether the maids of Bagdat would do any such eighteenth-century-English thing as 'verify a lay.' In these *Eclogues* Collins was putting new wine into old bottles, and frequently the wine smacks of the bottle.

72. song is the object of *bless'd* only.

ECLOGUE THE SECOND. (14)

The appropriateness of mid-day for this desert-picture is obvious.

1. boundless. By this change from the earlier text Collins at once removed a tautology (*desart waste*), and helped the reader to realize the immensity of the desert.

6. Mitford (in Dyce's *Collins*) compares Marlowe's *Hero and Leander*, sestiad ii, 11:

> Her painted fan of curled plumes let fall.

15, 16. It is incredible that a Persian, especially one competent to drive camels, should not have thought of the danger of winds, thirst, and hunger in the desert. The improbability is of consequence only because it lessens our sympathy with Hassan by lessening our sense of even an imaginative reality in the whole situation.

17. The personification seems unnatural here. Would not Hassan be much more likely to think of thirst as too inextricably a part of himself? An abstract Thirst, stalking the desert in search of an oasis, would hardly have troubled him. Contrast Shelley's *Revolt of Islam*, canto iii, stanza 31:

> Thirst raged within me, like a scorpion's nest
> Built in mine entrails.

20. A feeble conclusion. Not "tears and hunger," but death by slow torture, and bones bleaching on the sands, would be the pictures before Hassan's affrighted imagination.

21–28. As a delightful specimen of old-fashioned criticism the comment of Langhorne is worth reading:

> "It is difficult to say whether his apostrophe to the 'mute companions of his toils' is more to be admired for the elegance and beauty of the poetical imagery, or for the tenderness and humanity of the sentiment. He who can read it without being affected will do his heart no injustice if he concludes it to be destitute of sensibility." — Langhorne's *Collins*, London, 1765, p. 119.

Lines 23–26 are certainly pretty; rather too pretty to be spoken by a "wild" and "affrighted" man, in danger of death, talking to camels in a desert. But of course the poem does not aim at strict realism; and, further, Hassan may be thought of as half forgetting, for a moment, the horror of the present scene while recalling the "green delights" which he has foolishly left behind. Lines 27, 28, in which his thoughts return to the desert, deserve Campbell's praise : "He does not merely seem to describe the sultry desert, but brings it home to the senses." — Campbell's *Specimens of the British Poets*, London, 1819, vol. V, p. 310.

25. green delights. Dyce compares Thomson's *Summer*, 956 :

> And all the green delights Ausonia pours;

and Euripides's *Bacchae*, 866, 867 :

> χλοεραῖς . . . λείμακος ἡδοναῖς.

38. A bungling line : **thee** refers to *money* (l. 35) by a very abrupt change from the third person to the second ; **only** goes with *thee ;* **yet** apparently means *still, after all*, as so often in Elizabethan English.

40. fond = *foolish*.

52. One of the most imaginative bits in the *Eclogues*. Cf. the scene in *Robinson Crusoe* where Crusoe comes upon the footprint in the sand.

54. A piece of conventional imagery, made worse by contrast with the vigorous lines that follow.

56. "In Hyrcania and Curdistan, the woody parts of the country, wild beasts abound, such as lions, tygers, leopards, wild-hogs, jackalls, etc." — Salmon, vol. I, p. 334.

61, 63. "That part of the country which lies upon the Caspian and Hyrcanian sea is full of serpents, toads, scorpions, and other venomous insects." — Salmon, vol. I, p. 334.

66. Dyce compares Pope's *Epistle to Robert, Earl of Oxford*, 26 :

The lust of lucre and the dread of death.

71, 72. The punctuation in the Aldine *Collins* (a period after *won*, no mark after *Zara*) changes the sense. Both original editions have commas after *won* and *Zara*, indicating that *she* is the subject of *will be undone*, and *Zara* in apposition with *she ;* while *love* is the subject, not the object, of *won*, which has for object "whom" understood. The original punctuation makes the better sense : it is rather because Zara loves Hassan, than because he loves her, that she will be undone by his death.

73. **own'd the powerful maid,** *i.e.,* acknowledged the power of the maid.

ECLOGUE THE THIRD. (17)

The source of the *motif* in this eclogue is unknown. It is of course possible that Collins invented the story. Some have thought that he got the hint from a Persian tale printed in *The Free Thinker*, in 1719 (reprinted in Nathan Drake's *Gleaner*, London, 1811, vol. I, p. 272), but the resemblance is not very close. Cha-Abbas, king of Persia, took a great fancy to a shepherd lad, Alibez, whom he met on his travels. Alibez went to court, and finally became keeper of the royal jewels. But he still longed for the pastoral life and once revisited his early home. Under the next king he fell into disfavor and was ordered to give an account of his stewardship. Accordingly, he opened everything to inspection except one iron door. When this was forced open, nothing was found but "a sheep-hook, a pipe, and a shepherd's habit, which Alibez had worn, all of which he often took a pleasure in visiting privately, to remind him of his former condition."

There is no natural connection between the tale and evening. Apparently for this reason Collins wrote the introductory lines, which, though graceful, have no necessary relation to the story.

1. Georgia's land. In the days of the Great Abbas, Georgia was a province of Persia.

Tefflis'. Tefflis, or Tiflis, the capital of Georgia, is situated in a plain ; cf. *level green*, l. 2.

5, 6. These lines were added in the revised edition, no doubt to give a more distinctively Eastern setting, and perhaps also to lengthen the introductory passage, which, without them, is abrupt and manifestly a mere introduction; the added lines do much to make the prelude a pleasing and restful picture in itself.

17-19. "About Ispahan and some other towns jonquils grow wild: they have also daffodils, lilies, violets, and pinks in their season . . . ; but what they have the greatest quantity of are lilies and roses."— Salmon, vol. I, p. 332.

21. Collins doubtless had in mind the historical "Great Abbas," during whose long reign (1586–1628) the Persian Empire grew rapidly in extent and power; cf. l. 68 and the preface to the *Eclogues*. The real Abbas, however, was not at all the amiable innocent of the eclogue, but a cruel though able king, who put his eldest son to death.

"Shah Abbas enlarged the empire on every side; . . . he encouraged all arts and sciences; . . . he was also so severe against those who are guilty of the least fraud, that he ordered a cook to be roasted alive, and a baker to be baked in his own oven, for keeping of false weights. But with all his virtues I find Shah Abbas generally charged with cruelty, especially towards his son." — Salmon, vol. I, p. 343.

31. Mitford (in Dyce's *Collins*) compares Marlowe's *Hero and Leander*, sestiad ii, 5 :

> Yet as she went, full often looked behind.

And Dyce compares Cowley's *Country Life*, 17–22 :

> Unwillingly, and slow, and discontent,
> From his lov'd cottage to a throne he went.
> And oft he stopt in his triumphant way,
> And oft look'd back, and oft was heard to say,
> Not without sighs, Alas, I there forsake
> A happier kingdom than I go to take!

ECLOGUE THE FOURTH. (19)

The sense of midnight is limited to the beginning and end of the poem; there, however, it makes an effective setting for the dialogue.

1. Circassia, in the days of Hossèin, was one of the northern provinces of Persia, lying on both sides of the Caucasian mountains.

28. Dyce compares the *Georgics*, ii, 404 :

> Frigidus et silvis aquilo decussit honorem.

32-38. Collins got the material for these lines from Salmon. "Sultan Hossein succeeded his father, Sultan Solyman, anno 1694. This prince

chose to live an indolent, unactive life among his women in the haram."
The consequent misrule of his ministers stirred up to revolt, after some
years, Merewys, who "commanded four or five hundred tents on the
utmost boundary of the Persian Empire towards Usbeck Tartary." He
called in Tartars, Turks, and Muscovites, who, in the license of war,
overran Circassia and other provinces for their own advantage. "The
Muscovites surprised Derbent and Tarki [cf. l. 45], which lay next them
on the west side of the Caspian Sea. . . . The Persian ministry were
now in the utmost consternation. . . . They came, however, to this
resolution at length, to let the frontiers shift for themselves."— Salmon,
vol. I, pp. 318, 319. The capital of Persia was captured by the insur-
gents in 1722, and the shah was forced to abdicate. In l. 38 Collins
evidently sacrificed history to pathos, or else wished the reader to see
the situation as Secander saw it.

49. tents. *Seats*, in the text of 1742, was evidently a typographical
error; it is corrected in Collins's handwriting in the copy of the *Eclogues*
which he gave to Joseph Warton.

51. date. *Dale* was corrected in the same way.

56. Dyce compares Pope's *Translation of the Iliad*, xviii, 50:

> And the blue langi ' .h of soft Alia's eye.

The ingenuous Langhorne comments delightfully as follows:

" There is, certainly, some very powerful charm in the liquid melody of sounds.
The editor of these poems could never read or hear the following verse repeated
without a degree of pleasure otherwise entirely unaccountable : ' Their eyes' *blue
languish*, and their *golden hair*.' " — Langhorne's *Collins*, London, 1765, p. 132.

59. Georgian. Georgia was the next province to Circassia on the
south, and therefore likely to be next invaded.

71, 72. Mitford (in Dyce's *Collins*) compares the *Aeneid*, ii, 705, 706:

> Dixerat ille; et jam per moenia clarior ignis
> Auditur, propiusque aestus incendia volvunt.

AN EPISTLE, ETC. (23)

This poem was published in December, 1743 (see *The Gentleman's
Magazine*, December, 1743, register of books). In the following year a
second edition, much revised, appeared (see p. lxxix). Sir Thomas
Hanmer (1677–1746) was Speaker of the House of Commons in 1714–

1715; retired from political life in 1727; in 1743–1744 brought out his edition of Shakspere, in six volumes, which by no means deserves the praise Collins lavishes upon it.

5. doubts = *hesitation*, springing from self-distrust; cf. *fears* in the text of 1743.

5–8. The muse in these lines is not the same muse as in ll. 1–4; the former was the muse of poetry in general, whose are the myrtles blooming over Shakspere's grave, while the latter is the modest muse of the youthful poet. The inconsistency must be considered a blemish.

9–16. Only in brevity and the omission of the fulsome flattery of Hanmer is the passage an improvement upon that which it displaces in the first edition.

10. Science = *learning*. Collins ignores Rowe's two editions of Shakspere, in 1709 and 1714; Pope's, in 1725 and 1728; Theobald's *Shakespeare Restored*, in 1726, and his editions of Shakspere, in 1733 and 1740. Hanmer was much indebted to the labors of his predecessors, and says so in his preface; in fact Johnson mentions as one of his faults that " he supposes all to be right that was done by Pope and Theobald."

22. Phaedra's tortur'd heart. The allusion is to Euripides's play of *Hippolytus*, more especially to the early scenes, in which Phaedra, wife of Theseus, is tortured by her love for Hippolytus, her stepson, which she is ashamed to confess.

23. Œdipus, king of Thebes, ignorant of his real parentage, had slain his father and married his mother; on discovery of the truth, his mother hanged herself, and Œdipus, after putting out his eyes, became a wanderer on the face of the earth.

25. Dyce points out that the reading of the earlier text is almost identical with l. 35 of Pope's *Eloisa to Abelard:*

Line after line my gushing eyes o'erflow.

27–34 The plays of Plautus and Terence have great merit; Collins's praise of Latin comedy is therefore in a general way just, although no exact comparison with Menander is possible since only a few fragments from the latter's comedies have survived. Rome produced no great tragic poet.

33. Ilissus' laurels. The Ilissus flowed through Athens, the home of Greek tragedy.

35. As Arts expir'd, *i.e.,* at the downfall of the Roman Empire.

36. The priests of the Middle Ages ought not to be classed with the Goths and Vandals as the foes of learning; on the contrary, amid the dissolution of the old civilization the monks did much to keep art and letters alive. Collins is probably thinking, however, of the ascetic and dogmatic spirit of the medieval church as a whole, which was antagonistic to the joyousness and free thought of the classic world and the Renaissance.

37. Julius. Julius II, pope from 1503–1513, was a patron of art and literature; he laid the foundation stone of St. Peter's, and was a friend of Raphael and Michael Angelo. The Renaissance was of course a much more gradual growth than this line implies, its roots reaching far back into the Middle Ages; cf. ll. 38, 40 and the notes on them.

each exil'd maid. The Muses.

38. Cosmo. Cosmo de' Medici (1389–1464), one of the merchant princes of the Medici family who ruled Florence for many generations, was a magnificent patron of literature and art.

Etrurian shade. Florence, which is in old Etruria.

40. The soft Provençal. The troubadours of the south of France, who wrote in the Provençal tongue, were as a rule dependent for support upon the nobles whose courts they frequented; early in the thirteenth century many of them left southern France, then impoverished by the War of the Albigenses, and found a welcome in Italy and the north of Spain. The Provençal literature flourished from about the beginning of the eleventh century to near the end of the thirteenth. By his manner of referring to the troubadours, Cosmo, and Julius, Collins implies that their chronological order was just the reverse of what it really was. This could hardly be due to ignorance or carelessness; apparently it was occasioned by the wish to pass directly, for purposes of contrast, from Provençal poetry to Shakspere.

Arno's stream. Florence is on the river Arno.

41. wanton here probably combines the meanings of *sportive* and *loose.*

42. love was all he sung. This is not wholly true. The poetry of the troubadours also included didactic poems and tales of battle and adventure.

55. Johnson. Ben Jonson (1573?–1637), Shakspere's friend and fellow dramatist.

57. Fletcher. John Fletcher (1579–1625), who, partly in conjunction with Francis Beaumont, wrote many plays during the first quarter of the seventeenth century.

58. next in order. Jonson's first extant play was acted in 1598; Beaumont and Fletcher's earliest known drama was printed in 1607.

63. In his note Collins evidently alludes to this sentence in Dryden's *Essay of Dramatic Poesy* (the Scott-Saintsbury *Dryden*, London, 1892, vol. XV, p. 346): "They [Beaumont and Fletcher] represented all the passions very lively, but above all, love." In Collins's note, *their* apparently does not refer to Beaumont and Fletcher, since only Fletcher has been mentioned, but to Fletcher and Shakspere. Dryden, however, nowhere characterizes Shakspere after the fashion of l. 64.

64. This is a hard saying. It seems almost incredible that Collins, who found in Shakspere the inspiration for his delicate song about Fidele, could have meant what he seems to mean. But there is no escape. The obvious sense of the line is confirmed by *ruder passions*, l. 65, and still more by the fact that throughout the poem Collins alludes to male characters only except for a necessary incidental reference to the mother of Coriolanus. This curious verdict shows the tyranny of the age over the individual. It resulted from a survival of the Restoration ideals of gallantry and sentiment, which found Shakspere inferior to the more courtly Beaumont and Fletcher in the portrayal of woman and man's relation to her. Hence, in part, came the greater popularity of the latter's plays on the Restoration stage, and hence, too, the necessity which Dryden and his fellows felt, when revamping Shakspere, to "write-up" the love scenes. It should be noted, however, that Collins is praising Shakspere; and therefore the line should not be taken to mean that Shakspere had absolutely no feeling for woman, — strange praise for a dramatist, — but only that his chief interest was in those "ruder passions" which are characteristic rather of men than of women and are the staple of great tragedy. An opinion curiously like this is expressed by Joseph Warton in an article on *King Lear*, in *The Adventurer*, in 1754. (See No. 113; and the footnote to No. 140, in which the article is ascribed to Warton.) Warton says: "One of the most remarkable differences betwixt ancient and modern tragedy, arises from the prevailing custom of describing only those distresses that are occasioned by the passion of love. . . . Shakespeare has shown us, by his *Hamlet, Macbeth*, and *Caesar*, and above all by his *Lear*, that very interesting tragedies may be written, that are not founded on gallantry and love." The two friends may have discussed the matter together in university days; and if Collins shared Warton's opinion that the contemporary drama was enervated by excess of sentiment, it becomes easier to understand why he laid such exclusive emphasis upon Shakspere's delineation of the "ruder passions" of "man alone." Cf. the slighting reference to love as a predominant motive in poetry, in l. 42 and in the *Ode to Simplicity*, 37–39.

67–74. "Collins, dans cette épître à Hanmer, parle de la poésie française, de l'art dramatique français et de ses deux illustres représentants avec infiniment plus de mesure que Dryden, plus de sympathie sincère qu' Addison, et plus de justesse que Pope." — Émile Montégut, *Heures de Lecture d'un Critique,* Paris, 1891, p. 177.

67. The French drama reached its highest development about half a century later than the English.

Hardy, referred to in Collins's note, was born in 1560 and died in 1631.

71. Corneille, the greatest of the French dramatists, was born in 1606 and died in 1684.

Lucan's spirit. Lucan, the Roman poet (A.D. 39–65), wrote the *Pharsalia,* an epic on the war between Caesar and Pompey. His style, although uneven and bombastic, is energetic and occasionally sublime, and had a strong influence upon the style of Corneille.

72. The earlier reading is the better. *Full expression* and *Roman thought* characterize well the amplitude of language and Roman-like hardihood of spirit in Corneille's best tragedies; whereas *breath'd the free strain* is conventional and vague, and *he inspir'd* merely repeats *with Lucan's spirit fir'd.*

73. Racine (1639–1699), less bold and energetic than Corneille, was a more even and polished writer. The reason for not mentioning Molière probably is that his plays are not so good examples of that "correct" form which Collins is affirming to be a characteristic of the French drama.

74. chaster than Lucan; although it may mean merely *very chaste.*

75–78. The lines express the common view of Shakspere in Collins's day, that he was an irregular genius, lacking art, but unequalled in vivid naturalness ; see Pope's and Johnson's prefaces to Shakspere.

78. Th' historian's truth. The emphasis is upon the lifelikeness, not upon the accuracy. The second half of the line is a variant expression of the same thought.

manners. "By manners I mean whatever marks the characters of the persons." — Thomas Twining's translation (1789) of Aristotle's *Poetics.* Cf. *The Manners,* 41–52.

81. Henry's. The allusion is to Henry V.

83. Edward. Edward V, murdered with his brother in the Tower by his uncle, afterwards Richard III.

85. infant. This is poetical exaggeration ; Edward was a lad.

87. The line from Vergil (*Aeneid,* x, 503) is quoted incorrectly ; it should begin, *Turno tempus.* Turnus, king of the Rutuli, at war with the Trojans in Italy, has just killed Pallas and despoiled him of his belt inlaid with gold ; and the line contains the prophecy, fulfilled by the subsequent death of Pallas at the hand of Aeneas, that " Turnus will see the day when he would give a great sum to have let Pallas alone."

89, 90. See *King Richard the Third*, v, 3, 118–176.

95–100. The lines seem to refer, not to particular plays separate one from another, but to an Arcadie composed of features borrowed from all the idyllic plays. Collins was indulging in a species of poetical landscape gardening. Most of the elements, however, may be traced to their sources : l. 97 suggests *As You Like It* and *The Winter's Tale ;* l. 98, *A Midsummer-Night's Dream*, although the fairies met by moon-light, not twilight ; l. 100, *The Tempest*, although the time was August, not spring.

104. songs = *poetry.* There would be no propriety here in a special reference to the songs in the plays.

107, 108. Cf. *Ode to Pity*, 31–36.

108. Picture was formerly used as an abstract noun, where " Paint-ing " would be used now.

115, 121. It is singular that, with all Shakspere to choose from, Collins should select the subjects for both pictures from the Roman plays.

121. Collins's note evidently refers to this passage in Spence's *Dialogues :*

" And certainly what makes so beautiful a figure in the finest poets might deserve the imitation of the best painters. . . . If our Shakespear can give us the struggle of passions in the breast of Coriolanus, Wall might trace the same, and speak them as well with his pencil." — *An Essay on Mr. Pope's Odyssey, in Five Dialogues*, by Mr. Spence, Professor of Poetry in the University of Oxford, London, 1737, p. 81.

126. destin'd, *i.e.*, by Coriolanus to suffer the fury of war; cf. ll. 123, 124 in the text of 1743.

127, 128. The lines are not quite true to the spirit of Shakspere's scene. Volumnia, a genuine Roman matron, is reserved and proud ; she kneels, but as one who knows there is compulsion in her supplica-tion (see *Coriolanus*, v, 3). The earlier text was still farther from the truth.

137. Cf. *Aeneid*, iii, 445–451 ; and vi, 75, rapidis ludibria ventis.

139. no farther toil demand. These words are the perfection of unconscious irony.

140. just to nature, *i.e.*, restored to their original, natural condition.

145. some former Hanmer. Collins must have known that, accord-ing to ancient tradition, Pisistratus, the tyrant of Athens, was the one who brought together the Homeric poems. Perhaps he meant to imply that some unknown scholar really did the work under the direction of Pisistratus. In any case, he wished to flatter Hanmer by reducing the Greek editor, whoever he was, to a mere prototype of the English editor.

146. bo♦ndless is more significant than the earlier reading. It suggests how much was gained by bringing together these many and various poems into an "harmonious whole" (l. 141), while *tuneful* is an irrelevant commonplace.

147. his Athens. A graceful hint that Oxford University would gain lasting glory by this work of her son.

ODES. (33)

The *Odes* were published as a thin octavo in December, 1746, with the imprint 1747. For the title-page, see p. lxxx. "This Day are published, Price 1 s., *Odes on several Descriptive and Allegoric subjects*, viz. [The titles of the *Odes* follow in double column.] By William Collins. Printed for A. Millar, in the Strand; and sold by the Booksellers of Town and Country." — *The General Advertiser*, London, December 20, 1746. One thousand copies were printed: "Mr. Andrew Millar, Dr. Dec. 15, 1746. Mr. Collins's *Odes*, 8vo, No. 1000, 3½ shts." — Ledger of Woodfall, the printer, from *Notes and Queries*, 1st series, vol. XI, p. 419.

Pindar's lines may be translated thus:

> Skill to invent poetic phrase be mine,
> That so, a worthy servant of the Nine,
> I may drive onward in the Muses' car.
> Daring attend me, Power that knows no bar!

The appositeness of the motto is evident. The ode is an ambitious form of composition, calling for boldness, power, and originality.

ODE TO PITY. (35)

This ode and the next are companion pieces. Both were evidently suggested by Aristotle's dictum that tragedy effects, through pity and fear, the purgation of these and the like passions; and the drama is never far from the poet's thought. The conclusion of each ode indicates that Collins was intending to write a tragedy; cf. Johnson's statement, p. xviii. It was characteristic of Collins to offer up these odes on the altar of the tragic muse, as preliminary to a greater work which was never completed and probably never begun.

1-3. Cf. *The Passions*, 49, 50.

7. **Pella's bard.** Euripides died in Pella, the ancient capital of Macedonia.

The note by Collins is inaccurate. Aristotle's words are : τραγικώτατός γε τῶν ποιητῶν φαίνεται (*Poetics*, 13, 10) ; "he seems the most tragic at least of the poets." There is no special reference to Sophocles.

14. **Ilissus'.** The Ilissus flowed through Athens, where the plays of Euripides were acted and where he passed most of his life.

19. **wren.** The wren seems to have been selected as Pity's bird merely because of its gentleness.

thy myrtles. The myrtle, which in ancient times was sacred to the goddess of love and used for wreaths for bloodless victors, may appropriately be transferred to the gentle goddess of Pity.

20. **gentlest Otway's.** The tragedies of Thomas Otway (1651–1685) excel in pathos.

24. **Thy turtles.** The turtle dove, the bird of Venus by reason of its talent in courtship, may also be claimed by Pity for its gentleness. Collins is creating a new Pantheon in these odes, and his deified abstractions perforce filch from the old gods.

27. "In the *Ode to Pity*, the idea of a temple of Pity, of its situation, construction, and groups of painting with which its walls were decorated, was borrowed from a poem, now lost, entitled *The Temple of Pity*, written by my brother while he and Collins were school-fellows at Winchester college."— T. Warton's letter to Hymers (see p. xi).

41, 42. The lines are an interesting bit of contemporary criticism upon the prevailing intellectualism and lack of passion in English poetry of the period.

_____

ODE TO FEAR. (36)

4. **Fancy** = *Imagination*. Throughout the ode, fear as a mental fact (for Fear as a personification see note on l. 46) is not cowardice but imaginative and sublime apprehension of the terrible.

5, 6. The short metre helps to convey the feeling of alarm. The staccato movement in l. 5, and the repetition of *see* in l. 6, contribute to the same effect.

7, 8. The repetitions continue the impression of alarm.

18. near allied, *i.e.,* to the phantoms of l. 16.

22. In the note Collins has changed the case of the Greek words, perhaps to bring the phrase into the grammar of the English sentence. The order, also, is changed ; Sophocles wrote (*Electra,* 1388), ἄφυκτοι κύνες, "the hounds whom none may escape."

26. earliest Greece. The drama came comparatively late in the history of Greece ; Æschylus, the first of the great dramatists (cf. l. 30), was born in 525 B.C. *Earliest* perhaps is used, by rhetorical exaggeration, for "early"; or the comparison may be between Greece and later nations.

31. Æschylus fought in the battles of Marathon, Salamis, and Plataea. The stanza seems irrelevant unless the intention be to suggest again (see note to l. 4) that the fear invoked in the ode is tragic, imaginative, not cowardly : Æschylus, so great a master in the apprehension and portrayal of the terrible, was yet a brave man.

34. later garlands. Sophocles was thirty years younger than Æschylus.

35. Hybla's dews. Hybla, a city of Sicily, was celebrated for the honey produced in its vicinity. Sophocles was called "the Attic bee" because of the pervading grace and sweetness of his art. The implication that he left his usual manner for a harsher one in *Œdipus Coloneus* is not true. It is a characteristic of Sophocles that he harmonizes the terrible and the gracious; and, further, *Œdipus Coloneus* is less stern than *Œdipus Tyrannus* and some of his other plays.

37. baleful grove. The scene of the play is the entrance to a grove, at Colonus, dedicated to the Furies.

38. thy cloudy veil. The voice spoke from out a thunderstorm.

queen. Collins's memory was at fault. It was not Jocasta but a god: καλεῖ γὰρ αὐτὸν πολλὰ πολλαχῇ θεός, "For the god called him with many callings." — *Œdip. Colon.*, 1626, Jebb's translation.

39. son and husband. See note on *Epistle to Sir Thomas Hanmer*, 23. Translation of the Greek: "Now (when) no longer was their voice uplifted, silence befell. Then of a sudden rose the cry of one that called him. So all were struck with fear and sudden fright, that made their hairs to stand on end." — *Œdip. Colon.*, 1622–1625.

40. once alone. Another error; see "many callings" in note on l. 38.

46. weary lengths hast past. The excess of consonants and the unintentional rhyme are patent defects.

"Io seems to have been the original of this nymph." — Colchester edition of Collins, 1796.

Why should Fear be weary? And how should she " rest " by behold-
ing more horrors (cf. ll. 48–52)? The inconsistency is, however, as
Mrs. Barbauld (*Prefatory Essay* to Collins's poems, London, 1797)
pointed out, only incidental to a deeper one in the very conception of
Fear, who is thought of sometimes as suffering fear and sometimes as
inspiring it or delighting in it. Cf. *The Passions*, 17–20. The method
may, perhaps, be justified on the ground that the loss in unity is more
than offset by variety and completeness ; but the inconsistency should
not have been forced upon us by a mingling of the two conceptions in
one passage.

51. The spondees at the beginning and end of the line, and the alliteration in *big* and *beat*, make the line finely imitative of the pounding
of waves against a cliff.

57–63. Cf. *L'Allegro*, 100–116; *A Midsummer-Night's Dream*, iii, 2,
381–384; *Hamlet*, i, 1, 152–155 and i, 5, 11. Dyce also compares
ll. 60–63 with *Comus*, 43–46:

> Some say no evil thing that walks by night,
> In fog or fire, by lake or moorish fen,
> Blue meagre hag, or stubborn unlaid ghost,
> That breaks his magic chains at curfew time,
> No goblin or swart faery of the mine.

59. thrice-hallow'd eve. Apparently the reference is to Hallowe'en,
when fairies, imps, and witches are supposed to be especially active.
Cf. Burns's *Hallowe'en*.

70. cypress wreath. Not here the emblem of death, but Shakspere's
crown as a tragic poet.

71. The line is imitated from *Il Penseroso*, 175, 176 :

> These pleasures, Melancholy, give,
> And I with thee will choose to live.

ODE TO SIMPLICITY. (39)

1, 2. These lines are the key to the conception of simplicity throughout the ode : it is not a simplicity adopted as a manner, but the product
of naturalness and sincerity.

3. warmly pure, and sweetly strong. This simplicity, being the
product of nature, is free from the coldness and weakness of a formal,
academic simplicity. Cf. ll. 45, 48.

10. **decent** = *decorous, unpretentious in appearance.* Cf. ll. 8, 9 and *chaste, unboastful,* in l. 12. The conception is apparently an echo from *Il Penseroso,* 35, 36 :

> And sable stole of cypress lawn
> Over thy decent shoulders drawn.

11. **Attic robe.** Cf. note on l. 21.

14. **Hybla's.** See note on the *Ode to Fear,* 35.

16. In this ode in praise of Attic simplicity the allusion to the nightingale is pertinent, not only for the reason implied in Collins's note, but also because the nightingale is preëminently the " Attic bird."

18. **sweetly sad Electra's poet's ear.** The allusion is to Sophocles, one of whose tragedies is *Electra.* Milton (*Sonnet* viii) had used nearly the same words, " sad Electra's poet," to designate Euripides, who wrote a play upon the same subject. *Sweetly sad* should be taken with *Electra's :* in Sophocles's play (ll. 147–149) Electra, leading the chorus, mourns for her murdered father, Agamemnon, saying that the plaintive nightingale is more pleasing to her than such as forget the death of their parents; see the reference to the nightingale in Collins's note to l. 16.

19. **Cephisus** was the largest river in Attica, flowing past Athens.

21. **thy green retreat.** Athens. The reference throughout stanzas 3 and 4 is to Greek literature, as without equal in simplicity.

24. The period after *feet,* in the original edition, has been changed to a colon, because stanzas 3 and 4 seem to go most naturally with the first three lines of stanza 5, although they might be taken with l. 12.

26. **To** should be " into "; see *infuse,* l. 27.

32. **virtue's.** " Virtue " here has its original meaning of *heroic manhood.* The contrast is with effeminate love ; see l. 39.

35. **one distinguish'd throne.** The throne of Augustus, the patron of Vergil and Horace.

39. **her,** *i.e.,* Rome's. The reference is to the literature of medieval and modern Italy. Cf. *An Epistle to Sir Thomas Hanmer,* 40–44.

41, 42. The thought is that the natural advantages of Italy cannot win back simplicity to her poetry while she lacks the more manly virtues.

48. **meeting soul.** Cf. *L'Allegro,* 136–138 :

> Lap me in soft Lydian airs,
> Married to immortal verse,
> Such as the meeting soul may pierce.

ODE ON THE POETICAL CHARACTER. (41)

1. As once. The second term of the comparison is not reached till l. 17, where *thus* is correlative with *As*.

regard = *attention*.

3, 4. It is significant that Collins praises, not Spenser alone, but his "school." The romantic school of poetry, he says, is favored most by the Faerie Queene, whom he here conceives of as also Queen of Poesie. On the growing popularity of Spenser in the first half of the eighteenth century, see Phelps's *Beginnings of the English Romantic Movement*, chap. iv.

5. One, only one. In the note this one is said to be Florimel. Collins *had* read his Spenser "with light regard," or had forgotten what he read, for he makes two mistakes here. The girdle belonged to Florimel but could be worn by any one that had "the vertue of chast love and wivehood true" (*Faerie Queene*, bk. iv, canto v, stanza 3); and at the tourney Amoret, not Florimel, was the "unrivalled fair" who alone of all the ladies present could wear it (*Faerie Queene*, bk. iv, canto v, stanzas 16, 17, 19). Possibly Collins had a theory that Florimel and Amoret were really the same person. More probably his remembrance was hazy; and with characteristic indolence he made poetic capital out of his very uncertainty, and penned the first couplet instead of consulting *The Faerie Queene*.

7. Cf. *Il Penseroso*, 116–118 :

> And if aught else great bards beside
> In sage and solemn tunes have sung,
> Of turneys, and of trophies hung.

8. love-darting eye. Mitford (in Dyce's *Collins*) compares *Comus*, 753 :

> Love-darting eyes, and tresses like the morn ;

and Pope's *Elegy to the Memory of an Unfortunate Lady*, 34 :

> And those love-darting eyes must roll no more.

17–21. The excessive repetition of *to* harms the verse and somewhat obscures the meaning.

17. Young Fancy. Imagination, the source of all poetry, is forever young.

to me divinest name. This was no hollow conventionalism. To Collins, as to Keats, poetry was a passion.

18. whom. The antecedent is *Fancy*, not *me*.

19. cest = *cestus, girdle*.

23-40. The most obscure passage in Collins.   Mrs. Barbauld has expressed the thought as definitely as it admits of expression :

"Probably the obscure idea that floated in the mind of the author was this, that true poetry, being a representation of nature, must have its archetype in those ideas of the Supreme Mind which originally gave birth to nature." — *Prefatory Essay* to Collins's poems, London, 1797.

23. fairy legends. The allusion seems to be wholly fanciful.

29-31. The lines are not only anthropomorphic but disagreeably suggestive of *Jupiter Amans* or an oriental monarch in his seraglio.

29. the lov'd enthusiast. Young Fancy, l. 17.

32. sapphire throne. The blue heavens (cf. *vaulted shrine,* l. 33) ; but they are the upper heavens, above the "tented sky" (l. 26) of this world.   Cf. the cosmography of *Paradise Lost.*

39. rich-hair'd Youth of Morn. The sun.   Cf. the Greek conception of the youthful Apollo, god of the sun ; also *The Faerie Queene,* bk. i, canto v, stanza 2 :

> And Phoebus, fresh as brydegrome to his mate,
> Came dauncing forth, shaking his deawie hayre,
> And hurl'd his glistring beams through gloomy ayre.

40. subject = *lying under.*

was. One of Collins's few slips in grammar.

41-50. Collins's conception of poetry is significant.   Poetry is free from the evil passions ; is full of wonder, sublimity, and truth ; employs all the mental powers of man, and even has in it something of the angelic splendor.   Spenser and Milton evidently were the poets chiefly in mind ; cf. the references to them at the beginning and end of the poem.

46. tarsel's. The male falcon.

54. this hallow'd work. The cestus.   See ll. 5, 6, 17-21.

55. High on some cliff goes grammatically with *I view that oak,* l. 63.   The cliff is of course a symbol of Milton's poetry, and even the details are symbolic ; see especially ll. 56, 58, 59, 62.

57. tangled. A bold and picturesque word in this application.   It suggests the rugged, irregular contour of the cliff, whose shadows seem to lie in confusion along its sides and around its base.

jealous steep, *i.e.,* overhanging the valleys and apparently trying to seclude them from view.   Cf. *L'Allegro,* 6 :

> Where brooding Darkness spreads his jealous wings.

60. In its condensed richness the line reminds one of Milton's early manner.

63. that oak. An allusion to *Il Penseroso*, 59, 60:

> While Cynthia checks her dragon yoke
> Gently o'er th' accustomed oak.

66. spher'd in heav'n, *i.e.*, in one of the spheres in which the heavenly bodies, according to the Ptolemaic astronomy, are fixed. Cf. *Comus*, 2–4:

> where those immortal shapes
> Of bright aërial spirits live insphered
> In regions mild.

69. Waller's myrtle shades. The best poems of Edmund Waller (1605–1687) are his love poems, which in Collins's day were highly esteemed for their sweetness of versification. "Well-placing of words, for the sweetness of pronunciation, was not known till Mr. Waller introduced it." — Dryden's *Defence of the Epilogue* (the Scott-Saintsbury *Dryden*, London, 1892, vol. IV, p. 233).

> And praise the easy vigour of a line,
> Where Denham's strength and Waller's sweetness join.
>
> — Pope's *Essay on Criticism*, 360, 361.

Collins's preference for the more sublime and rugged poetry of Milton is one more proof of his dissatisfaction with the literary ideals of his time.

72. one alone. Milton. Cf. l. 5.

ODE WRITTEN IN THE BEGINNING OF THE YEAR 1746.

At the battle of Fontenoy, May 11, 1745, in the War of the Austrian Succession, the English soldiers with dogged courage exposed themselves to a terrible fire, and their column was torn in pieces. At Preston Pans, September 21, 1745, and at Falkirk, January 17, 1746, the English troops were defeated by the forces of the Young Pretender (grandson of James II), who claimed the throne of Great Britain. The ode may commemorate the English who fell in all these engagements. It seems, however, to have been occasioned by a particular and recent battle, and the second part of the title would point to the battle of Falkirk. But in Dodsley's *Collection of Poems*, 1748, in which the ode was reprinted, it immediately followed the *Ode to a Lady*, which was there said to have been "written May, 1745"; and the second ode was

announced as " written in the same year." If this date is correct, the
poem probably refers to the heroes of Fontenoy only. But the date
appears to be an unauthorized change or a careless mistake ; it contra-
dicts the date given by Collins in 1746, when he surely would not have
dated it so definitely, " in the *beginning* of the year 1746," unless his
memory had been clear upon the point.

The variant readings in lines 5, 7, 8 in some editions are without
authority.

" The following stanzas are almost unrivalled in the combination of
poetry with painting, pathos with fancy, grandeur with simplicity, and
romance with reality." — James Montgomery, *Introductory Essay to the
Christian Psalmist*, 1825, p. xi.

ODE TO MERCY. (44)

Dyce compares with the strophe Phineas Fletcher's *Purple Island*,
canto vi, stanza 16 :

> But see, how, twixt her sister and her sire,
>   Soft-hearted Mercy sweetly interposing,
> Settles her panting breast against his fire,
>   Pleading for grace, and chains of death unloosing :
> Hark ! from her lips the melting honey flows ;
> The striking Thunderer recalls his blows,
> And every armed soldier down his weapon throws.

A writer in *The London Magazine*, July, 1821, compares Statius's
Thebais, iii, 261–265 :

> Fervidus in laevum torquet Gradivus habenas,
> Jamque iter extremum, coelique abrupta tenebat,
> Cum Venus ante ipsos nulla formidine gressum
> Figit equos : cessere retro, jam jamque rigentes
> Suppliciter posuere jubas.

7–10. Cf. Joseph Warton's prose sketch of the Passions (see p.
118) : " She [Pity] frequents fields of battle, protects the slain, and
stanches their wounds with her veil and hair."

8. godlike chiefs alone. Probably a compliment was intended for
William, Duke of Cumberland, younger son of George II, who was
very popular at this time. Horace Walpole wrote of him, after the
battle of Fontenoy, " All the letters are full of the Duke's humanity and
bravery." — *Walpole's Letters*, May 24, 1745.

15. The Fiend of Nature. Apparently not War, but a principle of evil prompting man to war and other cruel deeds. The conception is vague; the phrase recalls the *Ode to Fear*, 18, 19, but nature must here include human nature as well as physical.

join'd his yoke, *i.e.,* yoked his steeds.

16. The allusion is apparently to the invasion of Great Britain by the Young Pretender.

17–22. The lines seem to refer to the dispersal of the Pretender's army by the battle of Culloden, April 16, 1746, and the consequent deliverance of Great Britain from the horrors of civil war. The picture might well have been suggested by the famous story that Attila, on his way to sack Rome, was met by Pope Leo the Great and persuaded to turn back.

26. queen is predicate nominative after *rule.*

ODE TO LIBERTY. (45)

3–6. The tradition is that the Spartans before entering battle combed and adorned their locks as for a festival. Probably there is in the lines a special reference to the fight at Thermopylae, where, it is said, the scouts of the Persians, peering into the narrow pass before the battle, were amazed and awed to see the little band of Spartans gaily combing their long hair.

4. "On ceremonious occasions the Spartans used to adorn their heads with hyacinthine chaplets. [See Theocritus, Idyl 18.] This custom probably suggested the comparison." — Colchester edition of Collins, 1796.

sullen hue. The classic hyacinth was dark-colored. Mitford (in Dyce's *Collins*) compares *Prudentii Carmina*, p. 492, ed. Delph. : Et ferrugineo vernantes flore coronas.

5. virtue = *manhood, valor.*

7. Alcæus. The poem quoted is a banquet song, preserved in Athenaeus. There is nothing to show that it is a fragment. Collins omitted six lines, two after l. 2, two after l. 4, and two at the end. There is authority for οὔπω, l. 3; but οὔ τί που makes better sense and metre, and is adopted in the translation below. By Hesychius the lines are attributed to Callistratus, not to Alcaeus. Certainly the Lesbian Alcaeus, who flourished about 600 B.C., did not celebrate the assassination of Hipparchus at Athens in 514. The metre is not even the so-called Alcaic verse.

Translation, including the omitted lines :

> In bough of myrtle I my sword will carry,
> As did Harmodius and Aristogiton
> That day the twain struck down the tyrant,
> And gave Athenians equal rights of freemen.
>
> Harmodius dear, thou hadst no part in dying,
> But in the Blessed Isles men say thou bidest,
> Where dwell (men say) the fleet Achilles
> And Diomedes, noble son of Tydeus.
>
> In bough of myrtle I my sword will carry,
> As did Harmodius and Aristogiton,
> When at the festal rites of Pallas
> The twain struck down Hipparchus the usurper.
>
> Wide as the world shall ever be your glory,
> Dearest Harmodius and Aristogiton,
> For that ye twain struck down the tyrant,
> And gave Athenians equal rights of freemen.

9. The assassination occurred at a festival of Pallas Athene, goddess of wisdom.

15, 16. Translation of the note : Nay, let us not speak of these things which made Demeter weep. — Callimachus, *Hymn to Demeter.*

17–25. The historical allusion is not apt. The overthrow of the corrupt and decadent Roman Empire by the northern barbarians, although an immediate blow to civilization and the arts, was ultimately a gain for freedom. Mitford (in Dyce's *Collins*) observes that the image is from Poggio's *de Varietate Fortunae.* Dyce quotes Gibbon : " The public and private edifices [of Rome] that were founded for eternity, lie prostrate, broken, and naked, like the limbs of a mighty giant." It does not follow, of course, that Collins's lines suggested Gibbon's figure, but the parallel is interesting.

19. The imitative effect of the line is due chiefly to the caesura in the last foot. Cf. an equivalent device in the *Aeneid*, v, 481 :

Sternitur exanimisque tremens procumbit humi bos.

26. the least, *i.e.*, of the fragments.

36. Science = *Learning, Liberal Culture.*

37. The Medici ruled Florence by methods curiously like those of a modern " boss " :

" It was impossible for Cosimo openly to assume the position of tyrant of Florence. . . . He managed to attain his object by means of the ' balìe.' These magistracies, which were generally renewed every five years, placed in the ballot bags the names of the candidates from whom the signory and other chief magistrates were to be chosen. As soon as a 'balìa' favorable to Cosimo was formed, he was assured for five years of having the government in the hands of men devoted to his interests. He had comprehended that . . . he who ruled men could also dictate laws." — *Enc. Brit.,* 9th ed., vol. XV, p. 785.

39. jealous Pisa. Pisa was annexed to Florence in 1406; became independent in 1494; after several attacks submitted again to her more powerful rival in 1509.

44, 45. Every year, on Ascension Day, the doge of Venice, with a magnificent ceremonial, symbolically wedded the Adriatic Sea, throwing a ring into its waters in token of the city's maritime supremacy.

47. Lydian measure. The ancient Lydian style of music was soft and amorous, suited to pleasant moods and subjects. Cf. *L'Allegro,* 135, 136:

> And ever, against eating cares,
> Lap me in soft Lydian airs.

49. The republic of Genoa, after a proud career as a maritime power in the Middle Ages, suffered many vicissitudes; it was taken by the French in 1684, and by the Austrians, with the aid of a British fleet, in the fall of 1746. This recent humiliation, no doubt, was what Collins had especially in mind.

53. The daring archer. William Tell.

55. The rav'ning eagle. Austria, from whose control Tell helped to free Switzerland.

58. Alva. The duke of Alva, the Spanish general notorious for his cruelty in the Netherlands, whither he was sent in 1567, by Philip II of Spain, to stamp out Protestantism there. He boasted that in the six years of his administration he had brought 18,000 persons to execution in addition to those slain in battle.

59. The revolted provinces of the Netherlands, through their commissioners, offered Elizabeth the crown in 1575, which she declined.

68. cliff sublime and hoary. An allusion to the high, white clay bluffs of the English coast where it faces toward France.

72. Orcas. The Orkney Islands (Latin *Orcades*).

wolfish mountains. In the Orkneys the sea-wall in places rises 1100 feet sheer from the waves, which howl in the caves hollowed out at its base.

75. her giant sons. "The island was then called Albion, and was inhabited by none but a few giants. . . . Among the rest was one detestable monster, named Goëmagot, in stature twelve cubits, and of such prodigious strength that at one shake he pulled up an oak as if it had been a hazel wand." — Geoffrey of Monmouth's *Historia Britonum*, lib. i, cap. 16, Thompson's translation.

uncouth, *i.e.,* causing alarm by its strangeness, a meaning that springs naturally from *unknown*, the literal signification of the word. **Strange** is doubtless meant to include the unnatural as well as the unusual. But, at best, *strange uncouth surprise* involves some tautology.

76. This pillar'd earth. Britain.

80, 81. Dyce compares *Comus*, 21–23:

> all the sea-girt isles
> That, like to rich and various gems, inlay
> The unadorned bosom of the deep.

82–84. " Both those isles still retain much of the genius of superstition, and are now the only places where there is the least chance of finding a faery." — Langhorne's *Collins*, London, 1765, p. 166.

85. thee. Liberty.

87, 88. The thought is that Liberty parted England from the mainland in order that, after being thrust out from Greece, Rome, modern Italy, etc., she might find a permanent home at last in this island fortified by the sea. It is only a poetic inversion of the truism that Britain owes her independence in good part to her insular position, as in the days of the Armada, when the seas fought for English liberty.

90. navel. Cf. *Comus*, 520:

> Within the navel of this hideous wood.

91. Oak groves were the Druids' favorite places of worship. The druidic temple may appropriately be called the shrine of Liberty, for the Druids took a leading part in the Britons' resistance to Rome.

93, 94. An unfortunate couplet. Even a " painted native " should have known better than to " meet " Liberty's " form celestial " with his " feet." It is a pity, also, that the exigencies of metre deprived *meet* of its " to."

103, 104. Mitford (in Dyce's *Collins*) compares Dekker's *Wonder of a Kingdom*, iii, 1, 18 :

> I 'll pave my great hall with a floor of clouds.

107. islands blest. The Happy Islands, where the souls of the heroic dead lived in bliss. See Lucian's *Vera Historia*, bk. ii, section 6, for the Classic conception of them ; and for the Celtic conception see A. Nutt's essay on *The Happy Otherworld*, in K. Meyer's edition of *The Voyage of Bran*.

108. Hebe, as the goddess of youth, may appropriately be coupled with Spring.

111. consorted = *in concert.* The Druids were poets and singers as well as priests.

118–120. Architecture is here sacrificed to symbolism, the mixture of Greek and Gothic signifying that ideal freedom ("the beauteous model," l. 106) combines all that is good in ancient and modern states.

122. sphere-found = *found in the spheres, i.e.,* in the heavenly spheres of the Ptolemaic astronomy, "beyond yon braided clouds" (l. 103), where this temple of ideal liberty is.

128. A proud claim that English freedom comes nearest to the ideal. Cf. ll. 61–63.

129–144. The passage contains several lines in Collins's worst manner; see especially ll. 131, 132, 141–144.

133–136. Cf. *Ode to Mercy.*

140. Cf. *Lycidas,* 68, 69 :

> To sport with Amaryllis in the shade,
> Or with the tangles of Neaera's hair?

ODE TO A LADY. (51)

The ode was first printed in Dodsley's *Museum,* June 7, 1746. It was reprinted in the *Odes,* 1747, and in Dodsley's *Collection of Poems,* 1748, 2d ed. The three texts differ considerably. The text of 1748 has been adopted in the present edition, except in l. 46 (see note). In 1748 Collins was living in or near London, in full possession of his faculties, and it is probable that the new text represented his latest revision of the poem. This probability is greatly strengthened by the fact that the changes are improvements, and especially by the unmistakable Collins flavor of stanza 4.

"I had lately his first manuscript of the *Ode on the Death of Colonel Ross,* with many interlineations and alterations. The lady to whom this ode is addressed was Miss Elizabeth Goddard, who then lived at or near Harting, in Sussex." — Thomas Warton (see p. xi). Warton goes on to quote several readings in the manuscript which differed from the published texts ; see the variant readings marked " MS."

3. fatal day. See note on the battle of Fontenoy, p. 103.

13. rapid Scheld's. The Schelde, or Scheldt, flows by Fontenoy. The epithet *rapid* is conventional and incorrect; from source to mouth the river has an average fall of only one foot per mile, and at Fontenoy it is flowing through the flat country of Belgium. Contrast Goldsmith's *Traveller*, 2 :

> Or by the lazy Scheldt or wandering Po.

19-24. The three forms of this stanza give an interesting glimpse into Collins's workshop. In the first form the element of grief for the dead hero is wanting, or, at most, is only implied. In the second form this element is added, but in the conventional expressions, "bath'd in tears" and "sigh thy name." Freedom, who in the first draft was Honour's superfluous double, gives place to "aërial forms," because two additional stanzas are now devoted to her farther on. In the last form the stanza is divided equally between the ideas of grief and honor. The superiority of the stanza in its final form is due chiefly, however, to the conception and expression. The second and third lines embody one of those delicate and shadowy fancies in which Collins most delighted ; the fancy is present in the text of 1747, but not fully developed. Honour is now conceived with more majesty; contrast "Imperial Honour's awful hand" with "applauding," "haunts his tomb," "bath'd in tears," or "sigh thy name." The same reserve of silent grief which appears in "bend the pensive head" is maintained in "point his lonely bed," and is especially grateful by contrast with the Honour of the text of 1747, who reminds one of the conventional maudlin lover. There is a slight gain also in confining the mourners to the vicinity of the tomb instead of letting them "rove . . . through every grove." *Thy virtues*, l. 19, helps us to remember that the ode is addressed "to a lady."

19. grieve = *lament.* This use of the word is rare but legitimate.

31. Edward's sons. Only the eldest son of Edward III, the celebrated Black Prince, fought at Cressy. The others were then children, nor were they ever famous as soldiers; John of Gaunt fought in later campaigns, but was not a competent general.

32. Cressy's laurell'd field. The Battle of Cressy occurred almost exactly four hundred years (Aug. 26, 1346) before the Battle of Fontenoy; 30,000 English defeated 100,000 French, killing 42,000. As Collins implies, the English troops at Fontenoy, although unsuccessful, fought with equal courage, attacking three times in the face of a murderous fire.

36. The two stanzas inserted at this point in the text of 1747 were wisely struck out in the next year. They lessen the unity of the ode by diverting attention from the death of Ross and the sorrow of the lady to the state of the nation. Collins may have added them as a compliment to William, Duke of Cumberland, younger son of George II, who defeated the army of the Young Pretender at Culloden, April 16, 1746, and freed England from what threatened at one time to be a serious danger. The victory was also an indirect blow to France, which had aided the Pretender, and for that reason was doubly pleasing to the English, smarting under their defeat at Fontenoy. The stanza reflects the universal feeling at the time toward the young duke, whose popularity was immense. Parliament voted him an additional income of £40,000.

"It is a brave young Duke! The town is all blazing round me, as I write, with fireworks and illuminations."— *Walpole's Letters*, London, April 25, 1746.

"Yesterday at Noon the Guns were fir'd in the Park and at the Tower, on Account of the Defeat of the Rebels ; immediately after the Bells begun to ring, and at Night there were more Illuminations, and greater Rejoicings, throughout the Cities of London and Westminster and Borough of Southwark, than has been known in the Memory of Man." — *The General Advertiser*, London, April 25, 1746.

46. **Harting's.** See Warton's letter, p. 109.

cottag'd. The reading of the text of 1748, *cottage*, seems like a typographical error; at all events its use here is incorrect.

ODE TO EVENING. (53)

This ode was first published among the *Odes*, 1747; reprinted, with changes, in Dodsley's *Collection of Poems*, 1748, 2d ed., and in *The Union*, 1753, which was edited by Thomas Warton (see Richard Mant's edition of T. Warton's poems, Oxford, 1802, p. xxiv). The text of 1748 and 1753 is followed in the present edition. It is improbable that Warton, an intimate friend of Collins and a careful scholar, would have adopted Dodsley's text unless the revisions had come from the hand of the poet. The changes are in Collins's manner, and most of them are improvements.

"I know he had a design of writing many more odes without rhyme." — J. Warton, quoted by T. Warton in his edition of Milton's *Poems upon Several Occasions*, London, 1791, p. 362 (note upon the translation of the *Fifth Ode of Horace*). T. Warton adds : " Dr. J. Warton might have added that his own *Ode to Evening* was written before that of his friend Collins."

In these days of painful searching for objective scientific standards in literary criticism it is restful to harken to the ever delightful Langhorne speaking on this wise:

"It might be a sufficient encomium on this beautiful ode to observe that it has been particularly admired by a lady to whom Nature has given the most perfect principles of taste. She has not even complained of the want of rhyme in it, a circumstance by no means unfavourable to the cause of lyric blank verse; for surely, if a fair reader can endure an ode without bells and chimes, the masculine genius may dispense with them."—Langhorne's *Collins*, London, 1765, p. 173.

"The very spirit of Poussin and Claude breathes throughout the whole, mingled indeed with a wilder and more visionary train of ideas, yet subdued and chastened by the softest tones of melancholy."—Nathan Drake's *Literary Hours*, Sudbury, 1798, p. 391.

"The ode is not so much to be read like a poem as to be viewed like a picture."—Robert A. Willmott, in his edition of Collins, London, 1854.

It is interesting to compare Joseph Warton's *To Evening*, published in the same month:

> Hail meek-ey'd maiden, clad in sober grey,
> Whose soft approach the weary woodman loves,
> As homeward bent to kiss his prattling babes,
> He jocund whistles thro' the twilight groves.
>
> When Phoebus sinks behind the gilded hills,
> You lightly o'er the misty meadows walk,
> The drooping daisies bathe in honey-dews,
> And nurse the nodding violet's slender stalk:
>
> The panting Dryads that in day's fierce heat
> To inmost bowers and cooling caverns ran,
> Return to trip in wanton evening-dance,
> Old Sylvan too returns, and laughing Pan.
>
> To the deep wood the clamorous rooks repair,
> Light skims the swallow o'er the wat'ry scene,
> And from the sheep-cotes, and fresh-furrow'd field,
> Stout plowmen meet to wrestle on the green.
>
> The swain that artless sings on yonder rock,
> His supping sheep and lengthening shadow spies,
> Pleas'd with the cool, the calm, refreshful hour,
> And with hoarse hummings of unnumber'd flies.
>
> Now every passion sleeps; desponding Love,
> And pining Envy, ever-restless Pride
> An holy calm creeps o'er my peaceful soul,
> Anger and mad Ambition's storms subside.

> O modest Evening, oft let me appear
> A wandering votary in thy pensive train,
> List'ning to every wildly-warbling throat
> That fills with farewell notes the dark'ning plain.

1. If. The conclusion begins in l. 15.

2. There is some tautology in *chaste* and *modest*, but on the whole the line was improved by the revision. In the text of 1747 the expletive *O* weakens the effect. *Pensive*, as Dyce remarks, was changed probably because it is used in stanza 7; and it is not so comprehensive a characterization of evening as *chaste*. Cf. *Verses Written on a Paper*, 24.

3. "'Brawling' was injurious to the deep repose of the poem; while the word 'solemn' substituted for an external fact a tranquil impression in the mind of the poet." — *Athenaeum*, Jan. 5, 1856.

7. brede = *braid, embroidery.*

9-14. Cf. *Macbeth*, iii, 2, 40-43:

> ere the bat hath flown
> His cloister'd flight, ere to black Hecate's summons
> The shard-borne beetle with his drowsy hums
> Hath rung night's yawning peal.

10. leathern wing. Dyce compares *The Faerie Queene*, bk. ii, canto xii, stanza 36, l. 6:

> The lether-winged Batt, dayes enimy.

Cf. the line from the poem written by Collins at school (see p. xiii):

> And every Gradus flapped his leathern wing.

11, 12. Dyce compares *Lycidas*, 28:

> What time the grey-fly winds her sultry horn.

24. flow'rs. The change from *buds* is a doubtful improvement. The rhyme with *Hours* is objectionable; and half-opened buds seem just the dormitories for elves — the same little creatures that in the days of Shakspere and Nick Bottom used to "creep into acorn cups and hide them there." But the picture of an elf curled up in a flower fast asleep, during the day, and tumbling drowsily out of it at nightfall to begin his pranks, is pretty enough for anybody.

29-32. The earlier form of this stanza is inferior in breadth of view; three of the four lines are devoted chiefly to the "ruin." It is inferior in tranquillity also (see *wild, dreary,* and *awful*), and therefore does not harmonize so well with the central impression of the poem. In the later form, *sheety* is a neologism, and does not please the ear; but it does picture the still and cool-gleaming surface of the lonely lake.

35, 36. "Like him [Milton] he has the rich economy of expression haloed with thought, which by single or few words often hints entire pictures to the imagination. In what short and simple terms, for instance, does he open a wide and majestic landscape to the mind, such as we might view from Benlomond or Snowden, when he speaks of the hut

> That from the mountain's side
> Views wilds and swelling floods."

— Campbell, in his *Specimens of the British Poets*, London, 1819, vol. V, p. 310.

47, 48. A figurative expression of the fact that the twilight in winter is short, evening quickly giving place to night.

49–52. The stanza is a serious blemish, especially as the conclusion of so beautiful and delicate a poem. The second version is the worse, but either is bad enough. The whole conception is conventional, and *sylvan shed* and *rose-lipp'd Health* are stock-phrases. What evening has to do with Fancy, Friendship, and the other capitalized ghosts assembled in the sylvan shed is not apparent, except in the case of Peace. Perhaps Collins meant to suggest that the evening is the best time for writing poetry, entertaining friends, and studying ; but this leaves Health unaccounted for.

49. the. The change to *thy* in the text of 1753 was apparently accidental, by attraction of *thy* in ll. 51, 52.

ODE TO PEACE. (55)

The ode was evidently suggested by the recent wars in Scotland and on the continent (see pp. 103, 105, 111).

1–6. Cf. the myth of Astraea, the goddess of justice, who left earth for heaven at the end of the Golden Age.

1. turtles, *i.e.*, turtle-doves, who draw the chariot of Peace.

5. The allusion is to the invasion of Great Britain by the Young Pretender.

10. the turning spheres. According to the Ptolemaic system of astronomy, the heavenly bodies were set in transparent hollow spheres having the earth as their common centre ; the revolving of the spheres produced ravishing music, too fine for mortal ear. Cf. Milton's *On the Morning of Christ's Nativity*, 45–48 :

> But he, her fears to cease,
> Sent down the meek-eyed Peace:
> She, crowned with olive green, came softly sliding
> Down through the turning sphere.

THE MANNERS. (56)

This poem stands somewhat by itself among the *Odes*. Its title would suggest that it is a companion-piece to *The Passions*, but the likeness stops with the title. The poem is more didactic and meditative than lyric. From the subject-matter it has been conjectured that the ode was written in 1743 or 1744, when Collins left Oxford for London; see ll. 1–6, 19–26, 75–78. The closing lines, in particular, are full of the exultation which a man of Collins's temperament would feel upon plunging, with a sense of newly acquired freedom, into the varied life of a great city. The style and verse also suggest that the poem is earlier than the other *Odes*, and more nearly contemporary with the *Epistle to Sir Thomas Hanmer*. Lines 67–70, with the foot-note about Le Sage's death in 1745, could easily have been inserted later, upon a report of his decease — a false report, for he did not die till November, 1747, and in Boulogne, not in Paris.

4. **requir'd** = *sought again and again.*

10–12. The thought is, that to prosecute such studies successfully one must subdue passion and folly — apparently a suggestive bit of autobiography about Collins's student days.

13. **porch.** " The Porch " is strictly the name for the school of Zeno the Stoic, because he was accustomed to meet his disciples in one of the porches of the agora at Athens. But the term is used here for Greek philosophy in general, with an allusion at the end to Plato.

14. **th' enliv'ning olive's green.** The olive was sacred to Athena, the patron deity of Athens, the chief seat of Greek philosophy. *Enliv'n-ing* seems to be merely pictorial, with no symbolic meaning.

15. **Science** = *Philosophy.*

16. **Fancy.** There may be an allusion to the poetic quality in Plato's philosophical writings, but more probably the reference is to philosophy in general as not consisting of pure reason, spite of its pretensions.

18. **Plato's shade.** The sly pun on " Plato " and " Pluto" is a neat climax to this passage of humorous criticism of philosophy.

20. **Observance.** This personification is the stillborn twin brother to *Opinion* in l. 8.

29. The more common thought is of art as a mirror, reflecting the realities of nature. Cf. Shakspere's "hold the mirror up to nature." Collins, apparently, was led into the figure by thinking of the world as a great spectacle, a phantasmagoria, in which things come and go independent of the gazer's will, as in the old magic mirrors.

36. social Science, *i.e.,* knowledge gained by mingling with society.

37–42. It is characteristic of Collins that he represents himself as no sooner observing the real world than wishing to retire and dream over what he has seen. The poet's sense for reality was slight. The whole poem is a dream of " Observation"; there is no real observation in it, and in fact it soon openly passes to literature. " When he speaks of studying the Manners, he had only laid down his *Plato* to take up *Gil Blas.*" — Mrs. Barbauld, *Prefatory Essay* to Collins's poems, London, 1797. But see the statement (p. xxviii) about his mimicking the peculiarities of certain persons in London.

44. The introduction of Contempt as a spectator, in addition to Fancy, is very sudden, and is merely a clumsy device for characterizing some of the manners.

45, 46. white-rob'd maids . . . laughing satyrs. The interpretation, in the Colchester edition of Collins, that the former are the virtues and the latter the vices, is more than doubtful. Satyrs were gross, earthy, but not exactly vicious. May not " white-rob'd maids " stand for the more spiritual characteristics of men, and "laughing satyrs " for their more earthly characteristics, merely natural and pleasure-loving but not necessarily evil ? The evil manners have been sufficiently punished already by Contempt's looking at them through her glass.

48. wild contending hues. In *contending* is apparently an allusion to the incongruity which is the basis of humor. *Wild* implies that the humor referred to is of a vigorous sort, closely connected with the passions ; cf. l. 49.

51, 52. Since humor, the thing, exists among all nations, the possession of the word "humour" is no reason for calling Britain a "favor'd isle."

55, 56. " The image of Wit is truly characterized. The mingled lustre of jewelry in his head-dress well describes the playful brilliancy of those ideas which receive advantages from proximity to each other." — Colchester edition of Collins, 1796.

58. In laughter loos'd. Dyce compares the *Georgics*, ii, 386: risuque soluto.

59–74. T. Keightley in *Notes and Queries*, 3d series, vol. XI, p. 350, pointed out that the whole passage is an invocation to Nature, and that consequently there should be no full stop until l. 74. In the original edition a blank space intervened between l. 70 and l. 71, but l. 70 ended with a colon; modern editions have aggravated the original error by changing the colon to a period.

59. Miletus. Collins fancifully turns the ancient city where these tales flourished into the author of them. The real author of most of them was one Aristides.

60. love-inwoven song. The tales were not song, but they were very much love-inwoven and highly indecent; so tradition says, for the tales themselves have perished. Collins follows Ovid in speaking of them as songs :

> Junxit Aristides Milesia carmina secum.
>
> — *Tristia*, ii, 413.

But a better reading for *carmina* is *crimina*.

61, 62. The allusion, apparently, is to the writings of Boccaccio (1313–1375), who lived much of his life in Florence, Tuscany.

changed, *i.e.*, from ancient Italy. Cf. *Ode to Simplicity*, 31–42.

63, 64. The popular notion was and is that chivalry, now become a sentimental and fantastic anachronism, received its death-blow from Cervantes (1547–1616), by his parody of it in the person and adventures of his lovable cracked knight Don Quixote. Cf. *Don Juan*, canto xiii, stanza 11 :

> Cervantes smiled Spain's chivalry away.

The real object of Cervantes's attack was not chivalry but the romances of chivalry, which were still read and admired and even believed by his countrymen. Chivalry as an institution was killed by the invention of gunpowder.

66. Castilia's Moorish hills. Valladolid, where Cervantes prepared the first part of *Don Quixote* for the press, is in Castile ; but the name of the province may merely be used for Spain. *Moorish* alludes to the conquest of Spain by the Moors in the Middle Ages.

68. watchet = *pale blue ;* see *blue*, l. 67. The color is suggested by that of the water in which the nymphs live. Cf. *The Faerie Queene*, bk. iii, canto iv, stanza 40, where the reference is to sea nymphs :

> Their watchet mantles fringed with silver round.

Dyce compares Drayton's *Polyolbion*, song v, 13 :

> She in a watchet weed, with many a curious wave.

69, 70. The allusion is to the story of Blanche (*Gil Blas*, bk. iv, chap. iv), whose father, from a sense of duty, compelled her to marry another, although she loved and was beloved by the king of Sicily ; her jealous husband, mortally wounded by the king, stabbed her as she held him in her arms. " At the time this ode was written the success of Thomson's *Tancred and Sigismunda* [1745] had probably made the story of Blanche . . . a favourite piece of reading." — Dyce.

71. Nature boon. In the Aldine *Collins* the line is wrongly pointed, with the comma after *Nature.* In the original edition the comma stood after *boon,* as the sense requires; *boon* is here an adjective, meaning " prolific." Cf. *Paradise Lost,* iv, 242, 243 :

> Nature boon
> Poured forth profuse.

Collins invokes Nature, the bountiful source of all truth, to inspire him as she had inspired Cervantes and the other writers mentioned.

THE PASSIONS. (59)

Wooll prints a prose sketch by Joseph Warton, " laid out by him as a subject for verse, at eighteen," which he thinks may have given Collins the idea of this ode :

" The subjects of Reason having lately rebelled against him, he summons them to his court, that they may pay their obedience to him ; whilst he sits on his throne, attended by the Virtues, his handmaids. The first who made her appearance was Fear, with Superstition, a pale-faced, trembling virgin, who came from Gallia, and was ever present at earthquakes, fires, sieges, storms, and shuddered at every thing she saw. Not so Anger, whose harbinger was Cruelty, with dishevelled hair ; and whose charioteer, Revenge, drove wheels reeking with blood. He himself stood upright, brandishing a sword, and bearing a shield . . . ; round his girdle he tied the head of an enemy just slaughtered, and his chariot was drawn by tigers. Next came Joy, chanting a song, crowned with vine leaves, waving a rod in his hand, at whose touch every thing smiled ; he was attended by Mirth and Pleasure, two nymphs more light than Napaeans : he was the institutor of feasts and dances amongst the shepherds, at a vintage, at marriages and triumphs. Then came Sorrow, with a dead babe in her arms : — she was often seen in charnels and by graves, listening to knells, or walking in the dead of night, and lamenting aloud ; nor was she absent from dungeons and galley slaves. After her Courage, a young man riding a lion, that chafed with indignation, yet was forced to submit. . . . He led Cowardice chained, who shuddered violently whenever he heard the horn [of Courage], and would fain run away. . . . Next came Æmulation, with harp and sword : he followed a phantom of Fame, that he might snatch the crown she wore : he was accompanied by a beautiful

Amazon, called Hope, who with one hand pointed to the heavens, and in the other held an optic which beautified and magnified every object to which it was directed. Pity led her old father Despair, who tore his grey locks, and could scarce move along for extreme misery; she nursed him with her own milk, and supported his steps, whilst bats and owls flew round his head. She frequents fields of battle, protects the slain, and stanches their wounds with her veil and hair. Next came Love, supported on each side by Friendship and Truth, but not blind, as the poets feign. Behind came his enemies, Jealousy, who nursed a vulture to feed on his own heart; Hatred also, and Doubt shaking a dart behind Love, who, on his turning round, immediately vanished. Honour, twined round about with a snake, like Laocoon. Then Ambition in a chariot of gold, and white horses, whose trappings were adorned with jewels, led by Esteem and Flattery. Envy viewed him passing, and repined like a pard with a dart in his side. Contempt, too, like a satyr, beheld, and pointed with his finger; but he too often reviled Heaven, whence plagues, pestilences, wars, and famines. When these were all met, Reason (sitting grander than Solomon), on whom the man Justice, and the woman Temperance, attended, thus addressed them." — John Wooll's *Memoirs of J. Warton*, London, 1806, pp. 11-13.

The wide difference between poem and sketch, both in central conception and in details, is evidence that Collins owed little to his friend's outline. But at a few points the resemblance is striking enough to make it probable that he had seen the prose sketch and took one or two hints from it. In both poem and sketch Fear is the first passion mentioned and Anger the second; Joy is masculine, is crowned with ivy, is attended by Mirth and another figure (Pleasure in the sketch, Love in the poem), and is associated with the dance; Love and Hate are both mentioned in connection with Jealousy.

T. Warton, in the note quoted in part on p. 111, says that a poem of J. Warton's entitled *The Assembly of the Passions* was written before Collins's ode; but there is no such poem among J. Warton's published poems.

17-20. Cf. notes (pp. 97, 99) on the conception of Fear in the *Ode to Fear*. Dyce remarks, "Perhaps he had an eye to the following lines of Sir Philip Sidney:

> A satyre once did runne away for dread
> With sound of horne, which he himselfe did blow;
> Fearing and fear'd, thus from himselfe he fled,
> Deeming strange euill in that he did not know."
> —Grosart's edition of Sidney, London, 1877, vol. II, p. 46.

26. sounds is either in apposition with *measures* (l. 25), or is governed by "with" understood.

35. The suggestion seems to be that Hope needs to be sustained by some response from without.

36. her sweetest theme, presumably, is love.   Including this line, the poem contains three allusions to love, and perhaps this was the reason why Collins did not give the passion more prominence in any one place.

43. denouncing = *announcing.   The Oxford English Dictionary* gives an example of this use of the word in 1718: " An approaching comet, denounced through every street, by the noisy hawkers."

75. oak-crown'd sisters. Wood-nymphs, attendant on Diana the **chaste-ey'd queen.**

93, 94. Dyce compares *Paradise Regained,* ii, 362–365; *Paradise Lost,* v, 286, 287; Pope's *Eloisa to Abelard,* 218 ; and Fairfax's transla- tion of Tasso's *Jerusalem Delivered,* canto i, stanza 14 :

> And shook his wings with roarie May-dews wet.

114. St. Cecilia was the reputed inventor of the organ.

115–118. Cf. the *Ode to Simplicity* for a similar expression of admira- tion for the simplicity of Greek art.

ODE ON THE DEATH OF MR. THOMSON.   (65)

James Thomson died on Aug. 27, 1748, at Richmond.   The ode was published as a thin folio in June, 1749 (see *The Gentleman's Magazine,* June, 1749, register of books; for title-page see p. lxxx).   The poem was reprinted in *The Union,* in 1753.

1. grave. In *The Poetical Calendar,* December, 1763, the reading is *grove,* which has been adopted in some editions.   There is no external authority for this reading, and little internal.   *Druid,* l. 1, might suggest " grove," but it does not follow that Collins wrote " grove."   *Sylvan,* l. 4, need not mean " in a wood," but simply " rural "; cf. *rural tomb,* l. 40.   *Shade,* l. 8, might refer to the burial grove, but the reference may be a general one to trees along the river's bank.   These are certainly insufficient grounds for rejecting as a misprint the reading of the two editions published during Collins's lifetime.   As internal evidence in favor of *grave* see ll. 31, 32, and l. 44, which is evidently meant to be a repetition of l. 1.

druid. The appropriateness of this designation for the poet of nature is obvious. Cf. *Woodland Pilgrim's,* l. 12.

6. harp. See *The Castle of Indolence*, canto i, stanzas 40, 41.

19. whit'ning spire. "Nor does there seem to be any local acquaintance with the scenery, for the church of Richmond is not white nor a spire, nor can it be seen from the river." — Mrs. Barbauld, *Prefatory Essay* to Collins's poems, London, 1797.

21. earthy. In Langhorne's *Collins*, in 1765, the word was changed, apparently by a typographical error, to "earthly." This reading, which has no authority and makes poor sense, has been reproduced in many editions down to within recent years.

26. pale shrine. Mrs. Barbauld, writing in 1797, said there was yet no monument to Thomson in the Richmond churchyard.

30. now, *i.e.*, nowadays ; in contrast with the poetical days of old, when water-nymphs found cool lodgings in the Thames.

31. Now, *i.e.*, at this moment. The use of the word in two senses in succeeding lines seems a slight blemish.

38. early doom is the language of affection ; Thomson was forty-eight years old.

AN ODE ON THE POPULAR SUPERSTITIONS OF THE HIGHLANDS OF SCOTLAND. (67)

This ode has had a peculiar history. It was not published during Collins's lifetime. The earliest public reference to it is the following sentence in Johnson's *Life of Collins*, in his *Lives of the English Poets*, in 1779 : "He showed to them [the Wartons], at the same time, an ode inscribed to Mr. John Home, on the superstitions of the Highlands ; which they thought superior to his other works, but which no search has yet found." The manuscript of the poem had been accidentally found, several years before, by Dr. Carlyle, a Scotch clergyman, who in 1784 read it at a meeting of the Royal Society of Edinburgh. In 1788 it was printed in the *Transactions* of the Society, with the following introduction :

"At a meeting of the Literary Class of the Royal Society, held on Monday, 19th April, 1784, the Rev. Dr. Carlyle read an ode, written by the late Mr. William Collins, and addressed to John Home, Esq. (author of *Douglas*, etc.) on his return to Scotland in 1749. The committee appointed to superintend the publication of the Society's Transactions, having judged this ode to be extremely deserving of a place in that collection, requested Mr. Alex. Fraser Tytler, one of their number, to procure from Dr. Carlyle every degree of information which he could give concerning it. This information, which forms a proper introduction to the poem itself, is contained in the two following letters,

'Letter from Mr. Alex. Fraser Tytler to Mr. John Robison, General Secretary of the Royal Society of Edinburgh.

'Dear Sir,

'At the desire of the committee for publishing the Royal Society's Transactions, I wrote to Dr. Carlyle, requesting of him an account of all such particulars regarding Mr. Collins's poem as were known to him, and which were, in his opinion, proper to be communicated to the public. I received from him the inclosed answer, and he transmitted to me, at the same time, the original manuscript in Mr. Collins's handwriting.[1] It is evidently the *prima cura* of the poem, as you will perceive from the alterations made in the manuscript, by deleting many lines and words, and substituting others, which are written above them. In particular, the greatest part of the twelfth stanza is new-modelled in that manner. These variations I have marked in notes on the copy which is inclosed, and I think they should be printed: for literary people are not indifferent to information of this kind, which shews the progressive improvement of a thought in the mind of a man of genius. [Mr. Tytler goes on to say that this is doubtless the poem referred to by Johnson in his *Life of Collins*. At Tytler's suggestion Mr. Henry Mackensie supplied the fifth stanza and half of the sixth.]

'I am, dear sir, yours, etc.'

'To Alex. Fraser Tytler, Esq.:

'Sir,

'I send you inclosed the original manuscript of Mr. Collins's poem, that, by comparing with it the copy which I read to the Society, you may be able to answer most of the queries put to me by the committee of the Royal Society.

'The manuscript is in Mr. Collins's handwriting, and fell into my hands among the papers of a friend of mine and Mr. John Home's, who died as long ago as the year 1754. Soon after I found the poem, I shewed it to Mr. Home, who told me that it had been addressed to him by Mr. Collins, on his leaving London in the year 1749: that it was hastily composed and incorrect; but that he would one day find leisure to look it over with care. Mr. Collins and Mr. Home had been made acquainted by Mr. John Barrow (the *cordial youth* mentioned in the first stanza), who had been, for some time, at the University of Edinburgh; had been a volunteer, along with Mr. Home, in the year 1746; had been taken prisoner with him at the battle of Falkirk, and had escaped, together with him and five or six other gentlemen, from the Castle of Down. Mr. Barrow resided in 1749 at Winchester, where Mr. Collins and Mr. Home were, for a week or two, together on a visit. Mr. Barrow was paymaster in America, in the war that commenced in 1756, and died in that country.

'I thought no more of the poem, till a few years ago, when, on reading Dr. Johnson's *Life of Collins*, I conjectured that it might be the very copy of verses which he mentions, which he says was so much prized by some of his friends, and

---

[1] Recent inquiries by the present editor at the rooms of the Royal Society, at the University of Edinburgh, and at the home of a surviving relative of Dr. Carlyle, near Edinburgh, have failed to discover any trace of the manuscript.

for the loss of which he expresses regret. I sought for it among my papers; and perceiving that a stanza and a half were wanting, I made the most diligent search I could for them, but in vain. Whether or not this great chasm was in the poem when it first came into my hands, is more than I can remember, at this distance of time.

' As a curious and valuable fragment, I thought it could not appear with more advantage than in the collection of the Royal Society.

' I am, sir,

' Your most obedient servant,

' Alex. Carlyle.' "

The *Transactions* appeared, evidently, toward the end of March. They were noticed in *The London Chronicle* of April 1–3, 1788, and in *The European Magazine* for April, 1788, which refers to them as "just published." A few weeks later there came out, in London, from the press of J. Bell, what purported to be a perfect copy of the ode as revised by Collins. This edition had the following preface and dedication :

" A gentleman who, for the present, chooses not to publish his name, discovered last summer the following admirable Ode, among some old papers, in the concealed drawers of a bureau, left him, among other articles, by a relation. The title struck him. The perusal delighted him. He communicated his valuable discovery to some literary friends, who advised him to publish it the ensuing winter. Mr. Collins, it would appear, by his great intimacy with Mr. Home, and his well-known predilection for Spenser and Tasso, made himself a master in the marvellous that characterized the rude ages. No wonder, then, that he paints the superstitious notions of the North so picturesquely poetical! By the public prints we are informed, that a Scotch clergyman lately discovered Collins's rude draught of this poem. It is however said to be very imperfect. The Vth stanza, and the half of the VIth, say the prints, being deficient, has been supplied by Mr. Mackensie. It has been published in some of these diurnal papers ; and is here annexed, as a note, for the purpose of comparison, and to do justice to the elegant author of *The Man of Feeling*. It is undoubtedly pretty ; but wants all the wild boldness of the original, which is certainly one of the most beautiful poems in the English language."

" To the Wartons.

" Gentlemen,

" The following Poem, being the long-lost treasure of your favourite Collins, is apology sufficient for dedicating it to you. Your mentioning it to Dr. Johnson, as it was the means that led to the imperfect first draught, so it likewise was the happy means of bringing this perfect copy to light. If the smallest poetic

gem be admired by you, how much more must you exult, on being put in possession of the brightest jewel, according to your own opinions, of your dear departed
friend? The world will no doubt, in this, soon join issue with you both, whose
talents do honour to your country.

> "Gentlemen, I am, with great regard, your Literary Admirer,
>
> "The Editor."

This anonymous edition came out, evidently, in May : it was reviewed
in *The English Review* for May, 1788, which was announced, in *The
London Chronicle* of May 27–29, as forthcoming on June 2. A second
edition appeared in 1789; but the editor still chose "not to publish his
name," and it is unknown to this day.

The anonymous edition did not escape contemporary suspicion, as
the following quotations will show:

"A person, ' who chooses not to publish his name,' has been lucky enough to
find this ode — after it had already been discovered in Scotland, and published in
the *Transactions of the Royal Society of Edinburgh!* The time of this anonymous gentleman's publication renders his story suspicious; and the internal
proof drawn from his edition of the ode will condemn him before every literary
tribunal. Wherever his ' perfect copy' departs from the Scotch prototype its
inferiority is *perfectly* conspicuous. This *faber imus* is unhappy in thus blend-
ing his lead with more precious metal; but industry is a commendable quality,
and the editor might have pressing occasions for the production of an eighteen-
penny pamphlet. . . . We consider literary imposition in a serious light; and
a cheat is not less so because he is a bungler in his profession. Even should this
editor alledge, with the needy apothecary, ' My poverty, but not my will, consents,' we must still consider him as a criminal." — *The English Review*, May,
1788.

"This is offered to the public as a *perfect* copy of Mr. Collins's beautiful ode.
If it is, indeed, complete, it is to be lamented that the *evidence* of its authenticity
is withheld from the public. Surely the gentleman, who found it in ' the
drawers of a bureau,' should allow his name to be published, and give us the sat-
isfaction of knowing whether it was in the handwriting of Mr. Collins; which is,
certainly, a material question. . . . The style [of stanza 5 and the first half of
stanza 6] does not seem, to us, to be in the manner of Collins." — *The Monthly
Review*, December, 1788.

But the text of the anonymous edition was adopted in Johnson's
English Poets, 1790; in Anderson's *Poets of Great Britain*, 1794,
although in his sketch of Collins's life Anderson expresses doubt of the
authenticity; in Park's *British Poets*, 1805; and in Chalmers's *English
Poets*, 1810, although, oddly enough, in a note to Collins's life in Chalmers's *Biographical Dictionary*, in 1813, the reader is warned against
the anonymous edition as "spurious." The only edition of Collins

which rejected the anonymous text altogether was that published at
Colchester in 1796 ; in this the *Transactions* text is followed, except
that the gaps are filled in by the editor himself.   The Geneva edition of
Collins, in 1832, left stanza 5 and the first half of stanza 6 blank, but in
the rest of the poem adopted the readings of the anonymous edition.
Mr. Swinburne, in Ward's *English Poets*, vol. III, with characteristic
abandon speaks of the ode as "villainously defaced ... by the most
impudent interpolations on record"; yet prints in the text many of
these same interpolations, ascribing some, vaguely, to "the later editions," and leaving others without any mark to distinguish them from
the original text.

The present edition, it is believed, is the first in this century to print
the ode in its fragmentary form.   The rejection of the generally adopted
text requires justification, although in the first instance the burden of
proof lay on the defenders of the anonymous text.

It is only fair to premise that a revised copy of the ode probably did
exist at one time.   The copy which the Wartons saw would naturally
be a revision of the first rude draught made five years before, unless
Collins's mental malady, which came on soon after, had prevented
revision.   And there is direct, although somewhat suspicious, evidence
that a perfect copy did exist.   Soon after the ode was published in the
Transactions, there appeared in *The* [London] *St. James Chronicle* [1] a
letter signed "Verax," containing the following extract from a letter by
T. Warton to Mr. William Hymers, whose papers Verax says he has
seen :

"'In 1754, I and my brother, Dr. Warton, visited Collins at Chichester, where
he lived in the cathedral cloisters with his sister.   Here he showed us an ode to
Mr. Home, on his return from England to Scotland in 1749, full of the most
striking superstitious imagery.   It was in his own handwriting, without a single
interpolation or hiatus, and had every appearance of the author's last revisal,
and of a copy carefully and completely finished for the press.   I offered to take it
with me to town,' etc. ....   On the whole [says Verax] we may conclude that
the Edinburgh copy is nothing more than a foul and early draught of this
composition."

This would be conclusive but for a singular circumstance.   This same
letter by T. Warton was published in *The Reaper* in 1797, and reprinted
in *The Gleaner* in 1811 (see p. xi); and the reprint in *The Gleaner*, at
least, does not contain the passage about the state of the manuscript,

[1] The letter cannot be found in the files of *The St. James Chronicle* in the British
Museum, from which several issues are wanting.   The transcript in Dyce's *Collins* has
been used in this edition.

although it purports to be the entire letter. Ragsdale's letter about Collins (see p. xi) was very carelessly printed in *The Gleaner*, and it is possible that Warton's letter suffered even worse; but the passage is an important and striking one, and if it really were in the original its omission is very singular. Furthermore, the two versions of the letter, even in the statements which they have in common, sometimes agree verbatim and sometimes agree only in substance, as the following excerpt from the letter as published in *The Gleaner* will show when compared with the above:

"The same year, in September, I and my brother visited him at Chichester, where he lived in the cathedral cloisters, with his sister. . . . Here he showed us an *Ode to Mr. John Home*, on his leaving England for Scotland, in the octave stanza, very long, and beginning, 'Home, thou return'st from Thames!' I remember there was a beautiful description of the spectre of a man drowned in the night, or, in the language of the old Scotch superstitions, seized by the angry spirit of the waters."

Some of the changes in Verax's version may have been made to secure clearness in the passage when wrenched from its context, as "In 1754" for "The same year." But others cannot be so explained; they appear rather to result from quoting from memory.

This curious state of things, taken in connection with the facts which are to follow, tempt one to a surmise which in the absence of proof must be put forth as a surmise only and not as a part of the serious argument against the genuineness of the anonymous edition. Is it possible that "Verax" and the anonymous editor were one and the same, some needy literary adventurer recently from Oxford, perhaps, who had there seen Hymer's papers? Did he, as Verax, quote loosely from memory for a few lines, and then forge the passage about the state of the manuscript? In brief, was the letter to *The St. James Chronicle* a clever advertising dodge, preparing the mind of the public for the appearance of the anonymous edition soon after?

The only bit of external evidence in favor of the anonymous edition — its dedication to the Wartons, and their silence — really amounts to nothing. Could the two brothers, now in their old age, be expected to remember the exact language of a long poem seen only once, thirty-four years before? On the other hand, the adverse external evidence consists of several particulars, separately inconclusive but cumulative in effect.

The times were favorable for such a forgery. Literary morals were lax and the critical spirit was comparatively feeble. Literary imposture was in the air. To mention only the more prominent cases, Macpherson's *Ossian* and the *Rowley Poems* of Chatterton had appeared less than a generation before, and had met, for a time, with encouraging success; while a few years later the Ireland forgeries were to be a nine days' wonder. There was no such presumption against literary imposture as obtains now.

The moment of the second text's appearance is suspicious. An imperfect form of a poem by a poet already famous is published and attracts considerable notice. A few weeks later, just in time to get the full advantage of this newly awakened interest, comes out another form of the poem, purporting to be the author's perfected copy. If the second form of the poem was really meant for a neat little stroke of business by some needy literary adventurer, it certainly could not have been better timed.

The fact that the edition was and remained anonymous tells heavily against it. If the editor had a genuine document, it is difficult to conceive why he should lurk in the dark. On the other hand, if he was an impostor, the motive for anonymity is obvious; awkward inquiries for a sight of the manuscript were thereby avoided. Especially, why should an honest man, with good evidence of his honesty, persist in uttering no syllable of defence after one prominent review had called for the evidence and another had branded him as a " cheat " and a " criminal "? If the statements in his preface were true, how easily, by the testimony of his " literary friends," the editor could have established the fact that he had had the manuscript in his possession months before the *Transactions* edition of the ode was published. Or, if the manuscript were in Collins's handwriting, as would be most likely, why did he not submit it to the Wartons for identification instead of merely dedicating his edition to them with politic flattery? This is what an honest man would naturally have done under fire. An impostor would as naturally have remained concealed. In the first edition the editor had intimated that his secrecy was only " for the present "; yet even the opportunity of a second edition did not tempt him to come out into the open, show his proofs, and refute his accusers.

The nameless editor's account of the finding of the manuscript is suspicious. It sounds like a sentence from a cheap romance. We have heard before of " old papers " and " concealed drawers of a bureau " and obliging " relations " who die and leave unexpected treasures behind. It is all too vague for truth. Who was the relative, what had been his connections, by what train of circumstances was it probable or even possible that one of Collins's manuscripts could have got into his bureau? Why is the manuscript not described? The preface suffers greatly if compared with the actions and letter of Dr. Carlyle. The latter found his manuscript among the papers of a friend who was also a friend of Home. He showed the manuscript to Home, who recognized it as Collins's. Later he read the poem before a learned society and submitted the manuscript to a committee of the society for inspection and publication. These are the words and deeds of an honest man with a genuine document. The preface of the anonymous edition and the course of the editor are of a different savor.

Further, the latter part of the preface contains deliberate falsehood, and is meant to mislead. The intention clearly is to give the impression that the editor has not seen the *Transactions* text of the poem. He has been "informed" by the "public prints" that a first draught of the poem has been found; it is "said" to be very imperfect; a stanza and a half, "say the prints," are missing, and Dr. Mackensie's lines, filling the gap, have been published in "some of these diurnal papers." The implication is plain that the editor knows nothing of the *Transactions* edition save what he has learned from the daily papers. The motive is obvious. If he has never seen the *Transactions* text, and yet has a manuscript identical with it, except for some revisions and additions, his version must be an original and not a forgery.

Now, in the first place, the anonymous editor would have had no difficulty in getting the first volume of the *Transactions*, which was for sale in London (see p. lxxxii). And, furthermore, the *Transactions* text of the ode, with the introduction and notes, had been reprinted in *The* [London] *European Magazine* for April. It is altogether improbable that a gentleman with "literary friends" should not have seen the newly discovered ode which even the daily papers were talking about.

In the second place, the anonymous edition carries plain evidence in itself that the editor had seen the *Transactions* edition, for he stole most of his notes from it. With a few insignificant exceptions, such as the statement that glens are valleys, his notes on lines common to the two editions contain no information not in the notes or introduction of the *Transactions* edition; and in several instances the plagiarism is obvious, the more obvious for the variations in the wording. The following instances are but two out of several about equally conclusive:

"On the largest of the Flannan Islands (Isles of the Hebrides) are the ruins of a chapel. . . . One of the Flannan Islands is termed the Isle of Pigmies; and Martin says there have been many small bones dug up there, resembling in miniature those of the human body." — Note to l. 142.

"One of the Hebrides is called the Isle of Pigmies, where it is reported that several miniature bones of the human species have been dug up in the ruins of a chapel there." — Note to l. 142.

"The island of Iona or Icolmkill. See Martin's *Description of the Western Islands of Scotland.* That author informs us that forty-eight kings of Scotland, four kings of Ireland, and five of Norway, were interred in the Church of St. Ouran in that island." — Note to l. 148.

"Icolmkill, one of the Hebrides, where near sixty of the ancient Scottish, Irish, and Norwegian kings are interred."— Note to l. 148.

In the second note, the anonymous edition follows the *Transactions* note even in an error. Martin really says (see p. 134) that *eight* kings of Norway were buried on the island, which makes a total of just sixty. But the anonymous editor, although he had only been "informed" by "the public prints" about the *Transactions* edition, by literary telepathy knew and adopted its mistake of *five* kings for eight, and neatly condensed its false total of fifty-seven into the phrase "near sixty."

Of course it does not follow that because the editor lied in one particular he lied in all. He might foolishly have tried to gain credence by deception for a genuine manuscript. But his deceitfulness in one point greatly damages his trustworthiness as a witness on the main question.

The internal evidence, on the whole, also makes against the anonymous edition.

It is a suspicious circumstance that, with thirteen exceptions, the later text differs from the earlier only where there were gaps to be filled. The exceptions are not only few but mostly trifling, such as a change from plural to singular; and in several cases they appear like corrections of what one man might take to be mere slips of the mind or pen in another man's work, such as *brawny* for *bony* (l. 51), *drooping* for *dropping* (l. 127), *helpless* for *hapless* (l. 135), and *scented* for *sainted* (l. 164). Now, we know from Thomas Warton that Collins was "perpetually changing his epithets." Is it probable that in this long poem his final revision of an imperfect first draught would show so few and so insignificant changes?

As to the quality of the new readings, some are adroit and not what one would expect from an impostor. Such is *skill* for *stile* in l. 138, a change which was not needed and which spoils the rhyme. Was it done for a blind? A bolder stroke is the conception of stanza 5, which turns away from the obvious line of thought, such as Mackensie followed in his substitute, and deals with history, especially with the battles of the Young Pretender. If this be forgery, it certainly is not commonplace forgery. On the other hand, could a shrewd forger do better than depart as far as possible from the thought in the verses already supplied by Mackensie, and so emphasize the contrast between the admittedly fictitious and the professedly genuine? Hints for the stanza might easily have been got from the *Ode Written in the Beginning of the Year 1746*, *Ode to Peace*, and the *Ode to a Lady*, all of which refer to the campaign of the Young Pretender, while the last contains a compliment to William, Duke of Cumberland, by name. (It may be remarked, in passing, that Collins would have been less likely to praise the duke in 1749 than in 1746. At the earlier date the duke's laurels were fresh upon him and his praise was in every one's mouth; at the later date he had recently suffered defeat in battle and his popularity was on the wane.) Furthermore, just as the *Transactions* edition supplied the anonymous editor with the material for most of his notes, so, curiously enough, the letter of Dr. Carlyle contains a sentence which might have suggested the subject-matter for the fifth stanza: "Mr. Collins and Mr. Home had been made acquainted by Mr. John Barrow, . . . who . . . had been a volunteer, along with Mr. Home, in the year 1746; had been taken prisoner with him at the battle of Falkirk, and had escaped, together with him and five or six other gentlemen, from the Castle of Down." On the other hand, it should in fairness be admitted that Home's participation in the war makes it more probable that Collins would allude to it by way of compliment to his friend.

Some of the new readings are rather pretty, and at least two, those in ll. 177 and 213, have something of Collins's characteristic manner. But, as will be shown soon, several of the best expressions do not fit well into their places, and none of them is beyond the skill of a clever literary adventurer, such as the editor probably was.

Still a third class of readings are wretched. Is it probable that Collins would have written, or at least would have let stand, in a revised copy, such lines as the following?

To monarchs dear, some hundred miles astray,
Oft have they seen Fate give the fatal blow!
The seer, in Sky, shrieked as the blood did flow,
When headless Charles warm on the scaffold lay!

In the first year of the first George's reign.

Hence, at each picture, vivid life starts here!

But argument from the merit of lines is hazardous, particularly as Collins's workmanship, in this poem and elsewhere, is uneven. An author is usually credited, however, with understanding his own thought. If, therefore, several of the new readings can be shown to imply a misunderstanding or an imperfect understanding of the thought, the proof will be pretty strong that the readings are not from the hand of the author. Now, it is a striking fact that in several instances the articulation of the new readings to the context is thus defective.

In l. 23 *bowl* is changed to *bowls*, apparently because the reviser thought, mistakenly, that one bowl would not do for "tribes." But in the next line *it* remains unchanged. *It* might possibly be taken to refer to *store*, but *bowl* is the more natural antecedent. It looks very much as if the anonymous editor forgot to change the context to match with his first change. Of course the error in revision might have been Collins's, but he is elsewhere scrupulous about his grammar, and, although often involved, is almost never incorrect.

In l. 107, *where hums the sedgy weed* is well enough by itself, but it does not complete the sentence; the verb which should govern *whom* (l. 105) and the verb's subject are both wanting. This is not like Collins. Compare the *Ode on the Poetical Character*, in which the syntax, although very complex, is very careful. Collins would never have left *whom* to its fate when it had straggled only two lines to the rear.

Line 177, in the anonymous edition, is pretty, but it would be more appropriate if the reference were to *A Midsummer-Night's Dream* instead of to the grim play of *Macbeth*. This objection loses force, however, if *fairy* be understood in its broader sense, as in *The Faerie Queene*, and if *fancy* be taken to mean "imagination." The more solid argument is that the inserted line does not harmonize grammatically with the context. It should be noted, in considering this point, that in the Carlyle manuscript there was no blank space between l. 176 and l. 178. The note in the *Transactions* edition says, " There is apparently a line wanting." Only by the rhyme-scheme was the omission discoverable, and perhaps Collins himself did not notice the irregularity or was indifferent to it; stanzas 12 and 13 were also each a line short, while stanza 2 had an extra line. At any rate, stanza 11 made sense and was grammatical as it stood in the manuscript. *There* refers to *historic page* and goes with *found*. The sentence thus ran as follows: 'There,' *i.e.*, in the old histories of Scotland, 'Shakespeare, in musing hour, found his wayward sisters, and with their terrors dressed the magic scene.' There was no hiatus in the thought, to be filled in later, as in the imperfect half-lines of the poem. Whether Collins, upon revision, would have inserted a line to make the rhyme-scheme regular, we cannot say. But if he had inserted a line he certainly would not have done it as it is done in the anonymous edition. For by the inserted line *there* is wrenched from its verb *found* and is left isolated and useless, its place in the new sentence being taken by *to those fairy climes*. This inserted line is not a careful poet's revision of his own work. It is a wedge thrust by a bungler into another man's sentence, which it rudely splits apart.

For the foregoing reasons the text of the anonymous edition is here dislodged from the place of honor which it has usurped so long, and relegated to the pillory of foot-notes, where it may be gazed upon by the eyes of the curious.

1. **H——**. John Home. (See Dr. Carlyle's letter.) Home was a Scotch clergyman, a friend of Blair, Robertson, and Hume. He came to London about the end of the year 1749, with the tragedy of *Agis*, which Garrick refused. It was at this time that he met Collins.

4. Home's tragedy of *Douglas*, after being declined by Garrick in 1755, was acted with great success on the Edinburgh stage in 1756. He afterwards wrote several other plays.

5. **that cordial youth.** John Barrow, by whom Collins and Home had been made acquainted. (See Dr. Carlyle's letter.)

17. **own thy genial land,** *i.e.*, acknowledge it as their country.

18. **Doric** = *simple, natural ;* cf. l. 33.

23. **swart tribes** are Brownies. Collins doubtless learned a good deal about the folk-lore of Scotland from Home himself; see ll. 184, 185. But he probably had read, very likely at Home's suggestion, M. Martin's *Description of the Western Islands of Scotland*, in which (London ed., 1716, p. 391) is a reference to the Brownie and the custom, in the Shetland Islands, of rewarding him for his work by pouring "some Milk and Wort through the Hole of a Stone, called Browny's Stone." But Collins must have been familiar with English folk-lore on the same subject, and especially with Milton's lines in *L'Allegro*, 105, 106:

> how the drudging goblin sweat
> To earn his cream bowl, duly set.

His indebtedness to Martin is more evident in later passages.

24–30. " A Spirit, by the Country People call'd *Browny*, was frequently seen in all the most considerable Families in the Isles and
North of Scotland, in the shape of a tall Man. . . .   There were Spirits
also that appear'd in the shape of Women, Horses, Swine, Cats, and
some like fiery Balls, which would follow Men in the Fields. . . . These
Spirits us'd also to form Sounds in the Air, resembling those of a Harp,
Pipe, Crowing of a Cock, and of the grinding of Querns : and sometimes they have heard Voices in the Air by Night, singing Irish Songs."
— Martin, pp. 334, 335.

39. had = *would have.*

48. shiel. " A kind of hut, built for a summer habitation to the
herdsmen, when the cattle are sent to graze in distant pastures." — Note
in *Transactions* edition.

57–69. " The Second-sight is a singular Faculty of Seeing an otherwise invisible Object. . . .   The Vision makes such a lively impression
upon the Seers, that they neither see nor think of anything else, except
the Vision, so long as it continues : and then they appear pensive or
jovial, according to the object which was represented to them." —
Martin, p. 300.

" Daniel Dow . . . foretold the death of a young woman in Minginis,
within less than twenty-four hours before the time ; and accordingly
she died suddenly in the Fields, though at the time of the Prediction
she was in perfect Health." — Martin, p. 321.

68. heartless = *dismayed ;* cf. l. 58.

118. As a feeble anticlimax the line is curiously like l. 20 in *Eclogue
the Second.*

121–124. Cf. Gray's *Elegy*, 21–24.

125–132. Mrs. Barbauld compares Ovid's *Metamorphoses*, xi, 654–
658 :

> Luridus, exsangui similis, sine vestibus ullis,
> Conjugis ante torum miserae stetit : uda videtur
> Barba viri, madidisque gravis fluere unda capillis.
> Tum lecto incumbens, fletu super ora refuso,
> Haec ait.

126. travell'd.   Cf. l. 122.

137. kælpie's. " A name given in Scotland to a supposed spirit of
the waters." — Note in the *Transactions* edition.

142–145. " There are also some small chapels here [on the island of
Benbecula]. . . .   The Natives have lately discover'd a Stone Vault
on the East-side of the town, in which there are abundance of small
Bones, which have occasion'd many uncertain conjectures ; some said

they were the Bones of Birds, others judg'd them rather to be the Bones of Pigmies." — Martin, p. 82.

146, 147. "At some distance south of St. Mary's is St. Ouran's Church [in the island of Iona]. . . . On the South-side of the Church . . . is the Burial-place in which the Kings and Chiefs of Tribes are buried. . . . The middlemost had written on it, *The Tombs of the Kings of Scotland;* of which forty-eight lie there. Upon that on the right hand was written, *The Tombs of the Kings of Ireland;* of which four were buried here. And upon that on the left hand was written, *The Kings of Norway;* of which eight were buried here." — Martin, pp. 260, 261.

155-171. "[St. Kilda] is the remotest of all the Scots North-West Isles : It is about two Miles in length, and one in breadth; it is fac'd all round with a steep Rock. . . . [The inhabitants] swear decisive Oaths by the Crucifix, and this puts an end to any Controversy; for there is not one Instance, or the least Suspicion, of Perjury among them. . . . They never swear or steal; . . . they are free from Whoredom and Adultery, and from those other Immoralities that abound so much every where else. . . . The Solan Goose is in size somewhat less than a Land-Goose. . . . The Solan Geese are daily making up their Nests from March till September; they make 'em in the Shelves of high Rocks. . . . The inhabitants of St. Kilda excel all those I ever saw in climbing Rocks. . . . This little Commonwealth hath two Ropes of about twenty-four Fathoms length each, for climbing the Rocks. . . . These poor People do sometimes fall down as they climb the Rocks, and perish." — Martin, pp. 280-295, passim.

169. tasteful toil, *i.e.,* appetizing toil, which makes even their "frugal fare" taste well.

173. gentle = *well-born.* The thought is that even an educated gentleman need not be ashamed to handle these popular superstitions. Cf. the apologetic tone of the preface to the *Oriental Eclogues.*

181-183. See *Macbeth,* iv, 1.

192-205. *Jerusalem Delivered,* by Torquato Tasso (1544-1595), was "done into English Heroicall verse" by Edward Fairfax in 1600. The following extracts (bk. xiii, stanzas 41-43, 46) will both explain the allusions in Collins's lines and enable the reader to judge whether the praise of Fairfax's verse is just; for Collins seems to be speaking of the translation and not of the original, perhaps because he thought the practice of English poets who had not disdained the "false themes" of the marvellous would have more weight with his friend than foreign poets could have.

He drew his sword at last and gaue the tree
A mightie blow. that made a gaping wound,
Out of the rift red streames he trickling see
That all bebled the verdant plaine around,
His haire start vp, yet once againe stroake he,
He nould giue ouer till the end he found
Of this aduenture, when with plaint and mone,
(As from some hollow graue) he heard one grone.

Enough enough the voice lamenting said,
Tancred thou hast me hurt, thou didst me driue
Out of the bodie of a noble maid,
Who with me liu'd, whom late I kept on liue,
And now within this woeful Cipresse laid,
My tender rinde thy weapon sharpe doth riue,
Cruell, ist not enough thy foes to kill,
But in their graues wilt thou torment them still?

I was *Clorinda*, now imprison'd heere,
(Yet not alone) within this plant I dwell,
For euerie Pagan Lord and Christian peere,
Before the cities walles last day that fell,
(In bodies new or graues I wote not cleere)
But here they are confin'd by magikes spell,
So that each tree hath life, and sense each bou,
A murderer if thou cut one twist art thou.
.   .   .   .

Thus his fierce hart which death had scorned oft,
Whom no strange shape, or monster could dismay,
With faigned showes of tender loue made soft,
A spirit false did with vaine plaints betray,
A whirling winde his sword heau'd vp aloft,
And through the forrest bare it quite away.

215. " Ben Jonson undertook a journey to Scotland afoot, in 1619 [1618–1619], to visit the poet [William] Drummond, at his seat of Hawthornden, near Edinburgh. Drummond has preserved in his works some very curious heads of their conversation." — Note in the *Transactions* edition.

219. Lothian's plains. The county of Lothian, in which Edinburgh is situated.

attend. In the Aldine *Collins* the punctuation is an exclamation point and a dash, which changes the sense. *Attend* is not in the imperative mood and addressed to " pow'rs "; it is indicative, and has *that* for subject. The first imperative verb is *lend*, l. 221. The *Transactions* text rightly had a comma after *attend*, although none after *plains*.